MISCHIEF
IN PATAGONIA

H. W. TILMAN

A picture of *Mischief* taken from the bowsprit: The oil drum on deck and the hills in the background seem to indicate that it was taken in the channels; on the other hand it is unlikely that in the channels one would see the prone figure (Procter) under the foot of the staysail sunning himself on deck

MISCHIEF
IN PATAGONIA

H. W. TILMAN

TILMAN
www.tilmanbooks.com

First published 1957 by Cambridge University Press
This edition published 2015 by Tilman Books
www.tilmanbooks.com
a joint venture by
Lodestar Books www.lodestarbooks.com
and Vertebrate Publishing www.v-publishing.com

Cover design by Jane Beagley
Vertebrate Graphics Ltd. www.v-graphics.co.uk

Lodestar Books has asserted its right
to be identified as the Editor of this Work

Series editor Dick Wynne
Series researcher Bob Comlay

The publisher has made reasonable effort to locate
the holders of copyright in the illustrations in this book,
and will be pleased to hear from them regarding
correct attribution in future editions

A CIP catalogue record for this book
is available from the British Library

ISBN 978-1-909461-16-1

Typeset in Baskerville from Storm Type Foundry
Printed and bound by Pulsio, Bulgaria
All papers used by Tilman Books are sourced responsibly

Contents

Photographs

Maps

Foreword

Sir Robin Knox-Johnston

MAJOR HAROLD WILLIAM 'BILL' TILMAN CBE, DSO, MC and Bar, is without doubt one of the twentieth century's greatest adventurers. War hero, coffee planter in Kenya, mountaineer and eventually a sailor, he led a full life anyone with an adventurous spirit can only envy.

He was born in 1898, and as for so many of his generation, life after school was an immediate posting to the trenches in France where the Great War was raging. Despite winning two Military Crosses for gallantry by the time he was twenty years old, he survived the slaughter that killed so many of his young, teenaged contemporaries, and such awards are a clear indication of a courageous person who is willing to take risks.

The war eventually ground to an end leaving a young man, barely twenty years old, who had already lived a lifetime of experience, with the question of what to do with a future he had not fully expected to have. In his first book *Snow on the Equator* Tilman wrote:

> To those who went to war straight from school and survived it, the problem of what to do afterwards was peculiarly difficult. A loss of three or four years upset preconceived plans, and while the war was in progress little thought was devoted to such questions. Not that there was no opportunity for such thinking, for there was ample time for that through solitary night watches at observation post or gun line; during periods of what was euphemistically called resting behind the lines; or, where most of us went sooner or later, in hospital. No, the reason was because making plans seemed rather a waste of time. Either the war would go on interminably, in which case one was already arranged for, or, in the other alternative, consolation

8

might be found in the philosophy of Feeble, that 'He who dies this
year is quit for the next.'

Fate made the decision for him, as he won a square mile of British East
Africa, now Kenya, in a lottery for ex-servicemen. He settled down to
coffee growing for the next twelve years, and might have continued if
he had not met Eric Shipton, another coffee grower in that country,
and was introduced to mountaineering. Over the next eight years the
two made some of the greatest climbs of the decade, and in 1936 he
achieved the first ascent of Nanda Devi, without oxygen, at 7816 metres
the highest mountain yet climbed.

Tilman volunteered in the Second World War, spending time with
Albanian and Italian partisans behind enemy lines, and earning a DSO
for his services, but was back climbing with Shipton in Tibet by 1947.
But by now the Himalaya were becoming crowded with expeditions
of younger men who could reach greater heights than was possible for
him as a fifty-year-old. However one suspects the real reason he looked
for pastures new was that the Himalaya no longer appealed to a man
who enjoyed the challenges of the wilderness, and exploring areas off
the beaten track away from the crowds. He was a natural pathfinder
and had always sought the excitement of seeing and climbing something for the first time. He decided to look further afield.

It was a conversation with a friend that led him towards the
Patagonian Ice Cap at the foot of South America. Areas marked *Inesplorado* would have been irresistible to a man of Tilman's tempera-
ment—and he did not resist. His first problem was how to get there.
He investigated taking a ship to Buenos Aires and crossing Argentina
but discovered that was not possible for two or three years. And so he
discovered the sea:

> There is something in common between the arts of sailing and climb-
> ing. Each is intimately concerned with elemental things, which from
> time to time demand from men who practise those arts whatever self-
> reliance, prudence, and endurance they may have. The sea and the
> hills offer challenges to those who venture upon them, and in the
> acceptance of these and in meeting them as best he can lies the sailor's
> or mountaineer's reward. An essential difference is, perhaps, that the

mountaineer usually accepts the challenge on his own terms, whereas
once at sea the sailor has no say in the matter and in consequence may
suffer more often the salutary and humbling emotion of fear.

Tilman decided to marry the two sports to achieve his objective. He
bought a dinghy, sailed in it and on friends' boats to build up experience, and then bought a 1906 Bristol Channel Pilot Cutter called *Mischief*. These sturdy boats, built for racing to ships to provide pilots, are
not the most manoeuvrable, but they were strong and cheap compared
with the cost of a new yacht at that time. He refitted her in Palma, and
arranged that the previous owner would sail her with him to South
America, although he insisted on bringing along his wife. Tilman,
who never married, gives the strong impression of being a misogynist,
and an insult to the wife's cooking led to husband and wife leaving
in Gibraltar, along with two other crew members. Now dangerously
short of crew he realised that by the time he had found replacements
it would be too late to sail to South America, and so resolved to sail
to England and await the next sailing season. A wise decision as you
don't go near Cape Horn in the southern winter in a small boat. He
found a scratch crew who mutinied off Oporto and then with one
or two friends who came out to join him he made a safe passage to
Lymington. It was not the best introduction to voyaging and we will
never know what caused crew to abandon the boat in such numbers,
but crew can be difficult unless they are willing to give and take, and
picking up bodies just to make up numbers is far from an ideal way
to gather in a good crew, unless they are outnumbered by competent
sailors to support the routine and discipline that is essential to the safe
and happy running of a boat.

His voyage the next year to South America to cross the ice cap
is one of the great sailing and exploration adventures. He describes
the passage through the Magellan Strait in straightforward terms but,
as those of us who have sailed in those channels know, it is a dangerous route with almost constant, cold adverse winds for the west-going
vessel, of Force 7 or more. Despite this he achieved his objective and
returned via the Panama Canal, a voyage of some 20,000 miles. In his
amusing style of writing he describes the vicissitudes in a casual way
that belies what he really achieved.

I have never been sure whether Tilman was particularly hard on his crews or he just chose them badly. Such comments about a crew member as 'felt that a man with the unseamanlike habit of wearing gloves at night in summer in the Atlantic would not prosper on a voyage of this kind' indicate a rather unsympathetic attitude toward his crew's comfort, even if one might share his surprise.

The bars of the waterfront and the yacht clubs are full of people talking about their experience and planned adventures, but all too often these appear to be imagined more than achieved or achievable. There is a harsh difference between the imagined demands of a voyage to high latitudes and the reality of working a boat in cold and clammy or gale conditions in the days before satellites, when navigation and the boat's exact position were never easy or precise. Sailing in old boats does make greater demands on the willingness to accept discomfort, or deal with recurring equipment failures that sap sleep and stamina, and many of Tilman's crews appear to have found this reality more than they could accept.

The loss of *Mischief* off Jan Mayen Island in 1968 has often been put down to Tilman's poor seamanship and in a way it is hard to put it down to anything else. A proper lookout, although appointed, was not kept, and he should have hove to further away from the coast, but it is easy to be wise after the event. The Arctic is an unforgiving place to sail and this was a bad year for ice. Once the boat had been put ashore, where the necessary repairs could be made, she was at the mercy of the weather conditions, and strong winds and ice floating into the bay eventually caused further damage that made the planned tow to Norway a forlorn hope. The strenuous effort for more than two weeks after beaching the boat, to patch her up, get her afloat again and sail to Iceland where repairs could be made would discourage most people. It is in his efforts to repair and re-float his boat that Tilman is at his best.

Sea Breeze's wreck off Angmagssalik on the east coast of Greenland is one of those nightmares every skipper wishes to avoid. In ice, engine failed, no wind, and the currents that push along the coast drifting the boat inexorably towards the rocky coast with no hope of rowing off: the conclusion was inevitable. Anchoring in that area is almost impossible. I tried it within the same fjord on one occasion but the drifting ice soon pushed our yacht so the anchor became trapped beneath an ice flow, from which we extricated ourselves, using the motor, with great difficulty.

Baroque, yet another Bristol Channel Pilot Cutter, nearly suffered the same fate close to Angmagssalik in 1975. She survived but all but one of the crew abandoned the vessel at Reyjavik. Tilman got her back to Lymington the following year and sold her and that was his last voyage north.

It is a part of his restless character that Tilman actively sought the unfrequented areas of the world. He relished the opportunity to explore, and the dangers that are inevitable to the pathfinder just brought added spice to his life. That Tilman completed so many of his voyages successfully is a credit to his determination and his seamanship.

The arrival of GPS has closed forever the heroic era of expedition travel, whether on land or at sea. It has deprived the modern sailor of the satisfaction of making a good landfall by use of the sextant or dead reckoning, and of the hours spent nervously watching out for a landfall in thick fog with just a lead line to indicate a possible position. So it is perhaps hard for the sailors of today to imagine the extra care and doubt that were a part of the navigator's lot until the 1980s. Tilman's voyages have to be seen in the light of small elderly boats, reaching out to Polar areas infrequently visited and not accurately charted, and with crews of varied experience, and without any of the modern aids that are now taken for granted.

I first heard of Bill Tilman whilst at the same school in Hertfordshire, Berkhamsted Boys School, which he had attended forty years earlier. He was a famous Old Boy who was still mountaineering at the time. To me his attractions were the adventures he made in far off places, which distracted me as I studied and dreamed in the same buildings in which he had been educated. Sadly we never met, one of my great regrets, so I know him only through his writing. But his writing is so amusing and comfortable and its subject is the real classic adventure that is not readily available to us today.

RKJ
May 2015

Preface

—◆—

THE APPROACH TO ONE'S CHOSEN MOUNTAINS is sometimes as interesting as the mountains themselves. Our approach to the mountains of Patagonia, by way of a sea voyage of some 10,000 miles, for the sake of traversing fifty miles of glacier, may seem a little long. So long that some readers may think there is an intolerable deal of sea, as it were, to but one halfpennyworth of mountain.

Once again I have to thank my old friend Dr R.J. Perring for criticising and correcting my slovenly writing. Those errors in grammar or good taste that remain may be confidently attributed to the author who, like other men, sometimes takes advice in order to do the contrary.

On behalf of the crew as well as myself I should like to acknowledge here the kindness of those many friends in South America whose names are not mentioned in the text.

H.W.T.
Barmouth
November 1956

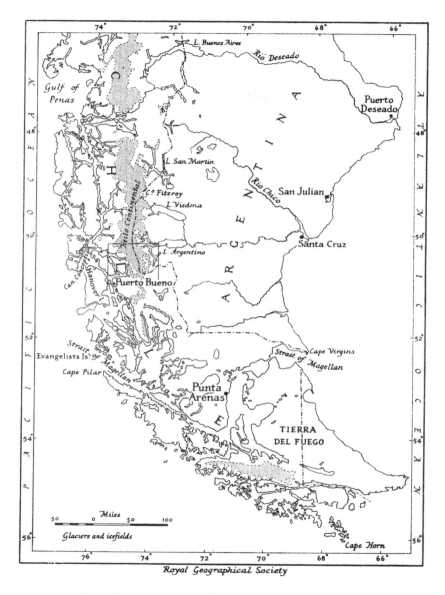

Map 1: General map of Chile and Argentine Patagonia
(Reproduced by permission of the Royal Geographical Society)

CHAPTER I

A FALSE START

We were a ghastly crew

THE ANCIENT MARINER

PROVERBIALLY IT IS NOT EASY to blow and swallow at the same time. So also it is not easy to combine mountaineering and sailing. There are, however, one or two places where such a thing can be done. In the Lofoten Islands a man can sail to the foot of his chosen rock face. On the southernmost coast of Chile, where the high Andes begin to dwindle, there are glaciers reaching down to the sea where a mountaineer can step from his boat and begin his climb at sea-level. A region such as this has an irresistible attraction for a mountaineer who, late in life, catches sea fever and aspires to making an ocean voyage in his own boat.

These Chilean glaciers have their origin in the Patagonian ice-cap (Hielo Continental as it is known there). This covers some 400 or 500 miles between 44° and 51° S., and varies in width from twenty to fifty miles and in height from 6000 to 10,000 ft. I first heard of its attractions in 1945, just after the war, from a friend who had learnt of it while a prisoner in Germany. For the most part the ice-cap was unexplored. No one yet had crossed it, and its glaciers, besides coming so conveniently down to the sea, had other strangely attractive features. Trees grew upon them—one felt this must be an exaggeration. Humming birds and parrots nestled in their branches and penguins paced the ice beneath. On the Argentine side of the range—the accepted way of approach—there were great lakes and forests, and beyond those to the east there were the rolling pampas where millions of sheep roamed, attended by gaucho shepherds, wild characters who lived on meat and maté tea, and rode down ostriches with whirling bolas. The more prosaic details of this glowing account were confirmed by the best map then available, the 1 to 1,000,000 sheets of the American

Geographical Society. This showed two white, blank spaces bearing
the magic word *inesplorado*. On these two blank spaces, the northern and southern parts of the ice-cap divided by the Rio Baker, were
shown numerous glaciers descending to the Patagonia channels on
the west, and to the great lakes of Argentino, Viedma, San Martin,
and Buenos Aires on the east.

This dazzling picture of a new field for mountain exploration had
its blemishes and the chief of these was the weather. Indeed, without
some such factor, there seemed little reason why such a large and
comparatively accessible region should remain not only unmapped
but also unvisited. A little had been done from the Argentine side,
for the most part by those interested in its geology and glaciology,
and since the lakes offered the readiest access most of the glaciers
descending to them had been named. As the prevailing wind and
weather are from the west, the Argentine side is more sheltered and
therefore drier and less windy than the Pacific side. Even so, of the
numerous attempts to reach the summit of the ice-cap or to cross
it (the first was in 1914) all except the most recent (1954) had been
repulsed by bad weather. The Pacific side, where the weather is worse
and where there is nothing but rock, ice, and tangled rain-forest, is
for nearly a thousand miles uninhabited and inaccessible except by
boat. This had scarcely been touched.

Neither my friend nor the fellow prisoners with whom he had dis-
cussed this exciting region were able to follow their ideas up, so that I
had to act alone. I must lose no time in getting to Buenos Aires whence
I could travel south and west by rail and bus; for there are roads or dirt
tracks across the Patagonian pampas serving the numerous estancias
some of which lie within fifty miles of the glaciers. At that time I had
no notion of crossing to South America in anything but the orthodox
way, but a round of the shipping companies soon showed me that there
was no getting there at all; or at any rate within the next two or three
years, by which time, perhaps, the claims of a multitude of would-be
travellers, all with prior or more urgent reasons, might have been met.
I forgot Patagonia and went back to the Himalaya.

In the decade after the war, thanks to the opening up of the
Nepal Himalaya, to the successful use of oxygen, and to the consequent scramble to be the first upon one of the giants, the tempo of

Himalayan climbing became fast and furious. In this decade the year 1949 was almost as noteworthy as 1953, the year in which Everest was climbed, for 1949 marked the throwing open of the Nepal Himalaya. That year one small and not particularly successful party went to the Langtang Himal. The next year saw a similar party in the field as well as the first big post-war expedition, the French party which climbed Annapurna I, the first twenty-six thousander to be climbed. In the autumn of the same year a party of four Americans* and the writer were the first outsiders to visit Namche Bazaar, the home of the Sherpas, and to traverse the Khumbu glacier at the foot of Everest. As if this was the ringing of the bell for the last lap the pace then quickened. With little or no encouragement from our account of what we had seen of Everest, European climbers, or rather nations, began to file their applications to attempt the ascent from the Nepal side; and at the same time numerous private parties set out for this wonderful new field. By 1953 the second applicant on the list (fortunately the British party) had climbed Everest. By 1956 not only had it been climbed again but the six next highest peaks had been, in the classic phrase, 'knocked off', and there were some forty expeditions afoot, eleven of them, employing 5000 porters, in Nepal.

The Himalaya are extensive, no less than 1500 miles in length, but a quiet man might well shrink from going, say, to Katmandu, the starting place for the Nepal Himalaya, if he thought he was likely to meet there eleven other parties with their 5000 porters. Moreover, if he had the misfortune to find himself travelling in the wake of one of these parties he would find food hard to come by, and local transport either unobtainable or at a premium. Such inhabitants as did remain would all be wearing climbing boots and wrist-watches and would drive uncommonly hard bargains. Added to these considerations is the undoubted fact that the Himalaya are high, too high for those who are not 'in the vaward of youth', and though the ageing mountaineer will assuredly find rich solace in its valleys and upon its glaciers he is not likely to resort to them when he knows there are peaks in other parts of the world still within his feeble grasp. So I began

---

*   Dr Charles Houston of K2 fame, his father Mr Oscar Houston, Anderson Bakewell and Mrs E. S. Gowles.

thinking again of those two white blanks on the map, of penguins and humming birds, of the pampas and of gauchos, in short, of Patagonia, a place where, one was told, the natives' heads steam when they eat marmalade.

Before this line of thought had led me anywhere I had acquired a stout 14ft. dinghy as a first step to venturing upon the sea. There are a number of mountaineers whose devotion to mountains is not entire, who own and sail boats; but there are few sailors who also climb. Of these, the best known was the late Conor O'Brien. He was a celebrated yachtsman who had designed his own yacht *Saoirse*. Having been invited to join a climbing party in the New Zealand alps for Christmas in 1923 he thought a voyage there an excellent opportunity for trying her out. Going by the Cape and running his easting down in the Roaring Forties he reached New Zealand. He arrived too late for any climbing so he sailed home by way of the Pacific and Cape Horn. One feels that his devotion to the sea came first and that in his eyes the loss of a climbing season was nothing to the accomplishment of such a tremendous voyage.

There is something in common between the arts of sailing and of climbing. Each is intimately concerned with elemental things, which from time to time demand from men who practise those arts whatever self-reliance, prudence, and endurance they may have. The sea and the hills offer challenges to those who venture upon them and in the acceptance of these and in the meeting of them as best he can lies the sailor's or mountaineer's reward. An essential difference is, perhaps, that the mountaineer usually accepts the challenge on his own terms, whereas once at sea the sailor has no say in the matter and in consequence may suffer more often the salutary and humbling emotion of fear.

The sea's most powerful spell is romance; that romance which, in the course of time, has gathered round the ships and men who from the beginning have sailed upon it—the strange coasts and their discoveries, the storms and the hardships, the fighting and trading, and all the strange things which have happened and still do happen to those who venture upon it. For the professional sailor this romantic veil has no doubt become threadbare, but for the amateur there is endless fascination. As Belloc says of the amateur sailor 'In venturing in sail upon strange coasts we are seeking those first experiences and trying to feel as felt the earlier man in a happier time, to see the world as they saw it'. With the mountains there is no romance. Man's association with them is relatively recent and perhaps artificial. With the sea it is as old as himself, natural and inescapable.

From the dinghy I graduated to a friend's four-tonner. In this we twice crossed the Irish Sea and these crossings had given us nearly as much satisfaction as if we had crossed an ocean. Even on those short passages we learnt a lot. We made unexpected landfalls; we lost a dinghy, we were sucked into and finally flung out of the Devil's Tail race near Bardsey Island—a chastening experience—and once in a thick mist we discovered in Cardigan Bay a buoy which no one else had ever seen before or has seen since. My apprenticeship was interrupted for eighteen months while I was in Burma but on my return I was lucky enough to be able to sail from Portsmouth to the Mediterranean in the 17-ton cutter *Iolaire* which then belonged to one whom, in seafaring matters, I have always thought of as the maestro*. Upper Burma is 500 miles from the sea and except near the Tibet border has no real mountains, so that on quitting it my unsatisfied longing was equally poised between mountains and sea. Naturally, therefore, it occurred to me to marry the two by sailing a boat to South America and landing on one of those remarkable glaciers to astonish the penguins and humming birds. Of course, I should miss the long and no doubt enjoyable approach over the pampas in the company of gauchos, ostriches, and whirling bolas, but one can't have everything.

This far-reaching decision was easier to make than even to begin to carry out. I had no boat and not much idea of what sort of a boat I would need. On that, no doubt, advice could be had, but had I a boat I had not the essential experience to handle it. The more I read, the more discouraging was the prospect. There were the gales in the South Atlantic and fierce tides in the Magellan Straits. The channels of Patagonia were beset with strong currents and stronger winds accompanied by incessant rain, sleet, or snow. The shores were uninhabited, inhospitable, iron-bound, and with more or less bottomless anchorages. It seemed wiser to buy a steamer ticket than a yacht.

---

*   Robert Somerset Esq. D.S.O.

The first and essential step was to find an amateur skipper who not only knew all about boats but who also would regard such a voyage, with its manifold difficulties and discomforts with eager enthusiasm. There were no doubt many such but would any of them have the necessary time? And how was I to find one?

However, in January 1954, I was put in touch with a man who was not only a competent and experienced sailor but also owned a boat of the right type. *Mischief*, built at Cardiff in 1906, was originally a Bristol Channel pilot cutter, 45 ft. overall in length, 13 ft. beam, and drawing 7 ft. 6 in. aft. Her register tonnage was 13.78 (by Thames measurement about 29 tons) and her displacement was about 55 tons, which meant that she was heavily built. Her only history known to me was what can be learnt from the entries in her certificate of registry. The first entry was in 1927 when presumably her life as a working boat came to an end and she was bought for conversion into a yacht. Since then she had had nine owners and her latest had bought her in Malta in 1953.

March had come by the time we had arranged for her to be hauled out for survey and, provided she proved sound, for subsequent fitting out. She was lying at Palma, Mallorca, where there was a good yard well used to building and repairing wooden ships. Another month passed before a slip was vacant. Time was short for if we were to reach the Patagonian channels by midsummer (southern summer), enjoy two months on the ice-cap, and be clear of those boisterous regions before the southern autumn, we had to be ready by the end of July. Everything turned on what the survey showed, for unless the hull was sound it was no use going on with the venture. To examine the outside planking the copper sheathing had to be stripped off. When this was done it was not worth putting back, but copper was so scarce in Palma that the yards and scrap-metal merchants fought for it and we got a very good price. The outside planking was mostly sound. Inside she had a foot of concrete ballast which filled the bays to the top of the floor. No doubt it had been put in when the boat was built and it seemed probable that if water had seeped beneath it the planking would be rotten. On the question of cement in yachts it is instructive to note the contradictory opinions of two experts. Claud Worth: 'The bays of *Tern* were filled with Portland cement which made her enormously strong and precluded decay in this region.' The Lonsdale Library *Cruising*:

'Cementing ought to be strictly avoided in a boat built of wood. The evils resulting from cement in the bilge of wood boats have been too often experienced. Moisture gets behind it and may result in dry rot.' *Mischief*'s cement had been well and truly laid. Amongst it were lumps of iron pyrites and the whole was almost adamantine. It took two men two days to chip out a hole a foot square in order to expose that small area of the bottom planks and keelson. Sure enough there was water. Overnight quite a pool collected and our hopes fell accordingly; but the yard foreman, who had spent a lifetime with wooden ships, having done some probing, declared the wood sound. In fact it was almost as hard as the concrete.

I bought the boat and we told the yard to go ahead with the refit. The several pages of our requirements had already been made out by my friend the late owner, to whose knowledge, thoroughness, and hard work I should like to pay tribute. As well as the work on hull and deck—new planks, recaulking, the doubling of all fastenings and keel bolts, new rail cap, stanchions for life-lines, and a hundred and one lesser jobs—all the standing and running rigging had to be renewed. In addition there was a mass of work to be done below—alterations to berths and lockers, the fitting of extra tanks for water and petrol, not to mention galley fittings, lockers for vegetables, sails, and bos'n's stores, rewiring, and so on. The mast had already been taken out for scraping and overhaul, as well as the inside ballast for chipping and painting. This consisted of about a hundred and twenty iron pigs of about 100 lb. each, vile things to have to handle and stow without the help of a professional weight-lifter. Inside ballast conjures up for most owners the dreadful vision of a ship on her beam ends with iron pigs cascading about the cabin. Happily *Mischief*'s ballast never shifted.

In May, after another cruise with the 'Master' in *Iolaire* to North African ports and Malta, I returned to Palma to live on board until we sailed. It was hard lying, for *Mischief* was still on the slip and as the ballast was still out there was no floor to the cabin. Work went on steadily but slowly. There were frequent interruptions for *fiestas*, but on the whole the Spanish shipwrights and carpenters worked well and the cost was half what it would have been in a home yard. At last the time came for her to go back into the water. We slapped on the blue anti-fouling paint with a will and when she was afloat she was moored alongside a floating crane where the mast was stepped and the rigging set up. There were still hundreds of small things to be done before she was ready for sea, but now she was looking like a ship, and a deep sea ship at that, with the after shrouds and the topping lifts swathed in baggywrinkle. The shrouds were the admiration of all. Later they raised many a laugh in yachting harbours, for they were of unyachtlike dimensions, 2½in. wire with bottle screws to match. The forestay was 2¾in. wire and the rest of the standing and running rigging was proportionately sturdy. It paid handsomely. We never need have anxiety about the mast, nothing ever carried away, and we returned to England in 1956 using the same main sheet and jib sheets we had fitted at Palma. Altogether one felt that she was 'fit to shunt ice' as the old whaling captain remarked to Slocum of his famous *Spray*. Though we did not encounter any storm such as drove *Spray* back willy-nilly into the Magellan Straits, we did in fact shunt a great deal of ice, something which *Spray* never had to do.

The new suit of sails having arrived from England, the mainsail was bent on, and at the end of July, late but not too late, we left Mallorca bound for Gibraltar where we had to pick up sea stores sent there from England. These consisted of food for six months. A like amount had been sent to Montevideo to await our arrival. In contrast to my subsequent experience a crew had been found without much effort on my part. As they dispersed with equal facility there is no need to name them. When agreeing with the previous owner that he would skipper *Mischief* for me, an ineluctable condition (on his part) was that his wife should be one of the crew. She was a modern Grace Darling who could hand, reef, and steer, as the phrase goes, and she shipped as bos'n. I had had misgivings about this, not that I questioned her ability but I had at the back of my mind the remark of some sage from China, a country prolific in sages, to the effect that discord is not sent down from Heaven but is brought about by women. But it was both or nothing; no song, no supper.

We made a slow passage of ten days to Gibraltar where we had no sooner tied up than I learnt that the skipper and his wife were going no farther. On passage, relations between Grace Darling and myself had been strained although I had been self-effacing, as an owner should be, and as silent as usual. Perhaps one of the few remarks I ventured had not been well chosen. We took it in turns to cook and the day after Grace Darling's turn, when one of the crew who knew how to cook was officiating, I thanked God aloud for having on board one whose presence ensured our having good meals on at least one day in five. Besides a clash of temperaments there may have been other factors; we were late in starting, were bound for a rude climate, and in spite of all that had been done we were not in every respect ready for sea. With a mind fully occupied with all the implications of this miserable, unlooked-for, and abrupt ending to a promising venture, I could yet feel for the skipper whose hard work in fitting out now went for nothing. But he had no option—a wife's counsel is bad, but he who will not take it is mad.

The other two crew members adjourned immediately to the Yacht Club to celebrate our safe arrival, and it soon became clear that they had no intention of continuing. Neither would they help take the ship back to England although one of them was well able to take charge of a yacht. I could not leave her at Gibraltar where there are land rats and water rats who prey upon laid-up ships, so the only thing to do was to sail her back with a scratch crew. To add to these embarrassments I had to explain to the admiral who had honoured the venture by asking the crew and myself to lunch that we were no longer on speaking terms. On the other hand it was pleasant to be joined the same day by David Drummond, lately an instructor at the Outward Bound Mountain School, Eskdale, who had hoped to be one of the ice-cap party. He knew nothing about the sea but being a mountaineer he would stand by me and not desert like the yachtsmen.

September was well advanced before we cleared from Gibraltar with a scratch crew—the exotic fruits of an advertisement in the local newspaper. The only two who counted were a sergeant and a corporal from a R.A.S.C. Water Transport unit who had obtained a month's leave in order to come—a month, I thought in my innocence, being ample allowance for a voyage of 1200 odd miles. They had been to sea but knew nothing about sail. They soon picked it up, were a likeable pair, and failed only in staying power. A private from the Duke of Wellington's, and a Scottish youth from the dockyard who had come out three weeks before and now wanted to go home, completed the motley crew and irritated beyond measure the novice who was now skipper. In summer strong northerly winds prevail along the Portuguese coast.

By late September these should have weakened and have become less steady. I counted on having at least a small proportion of fair winds, but having rounded Cape St Vincent in good style we met with constant, strong head winds with which we battled for the next eighteen days. By going out a hundred miles from the coast we fared no better and succeeded only in demoralising the crew, who would have much preferred noting our progress, however slow, against some land. Having no sextant I was navigating by dead reckoning but thanks mainly to a very friendly Union Castle boat, the *Roxburgh Castle*, I had a pretty good idea where we were. The incessant beating into wind and sea, with one or two nights spent hove to, told on the crew who began to murmur loudly. Unwisely, perhaps, I had told them we were about the latitude of Oporto, whereupon the two N.C.O.s declared that unless I put in and landed them they would no longer stand their watches. In fact, mutiny on the high seas. The situation called for a bucko mate and a belaying pin. I had plenty of belaying pins (there were half a dozen each side in the fife-rail) but no bucko mate. I was too old for the role and David was too good-natured. Having little confidence in myself and none in the crew Oporto was the last place I should have picked upon. At the entrance is a bar, the tidal streams attain a rate of seven knots, and during freshets the ebb in the river has been reported to run at sixteen knots.

There was nothing else for it so I headed her for Oporto where we made a good landfall. By sundown we were off the bar. A swell was running and we had no information as to the state of the tide. On board were Tide Tables for all the ports of the South Atlantic, the Pacific, and the Mediterranean, but none for the coast of Portugal. As we motored slowly in we were startled by the report of a cannon. Were the natives hostile or was it an old Portuguese custom thus to salute the setting sun? A moment later a man appeared on the jetty beyond the bar excitedly waving a newspaper. The sergeant assured me he was beckoning us in whereas I was quite sure he was waving us out. Even as I put her round she bumped twice on the bottom. We anchored for the night well outside the bar.

In the morning a pilot came off, took us up the river and moored us below the city with warps, springs, and our heaviest anchor. He said they had fired the gun to warn us and that had we attempted to cross the bar we would surely have lost the ship. The R.A.S.C. men departed, leaving me with three weak hands, two of them unwilling. I had to choose between the cheap but doubtful step of recruiting two unknown Portuguese sailors, with whom I should not be able to exchange a word, or the expensive step of calling for professional help from home. Lying in a nearby yard with a professional skipper on board was the English yacht *Iyruna* which had left Gibraltar just before us. She had met heavy weather, been damaged, and had put back to lay up for the winter. Her skipper was not able to come but he gave me the name of a likely amateur, W. A. Procter (of whom more later) who at that time, however, could not leave England. At length Humphrey Barton and a friend flew out and we sailed the same afternoon.

By now, late October, our old enemy the north wind had given place to south-westerly winds with drizzling rain. Although the wind was not strong we managed to break the gaff. This decided us to put into Vigo. We were off what we thought was the entrance to the bay. It was dusk, the weather thick, and we attributed to low cloud the fact that we could not see the light, which, as in many Spanish lighthouses, is sited too high. *Mischief* had now a skipper of very different calibre, so we stood boldly in and once inside the narrow entrance picked up the buoys marking the channel. For two hours we motored on towards the bright lights of a large town and having closed the lights and duly noted the wharves where, I was assured, Atlantic liners tie up, we began searching for the Yacht Club. Although we went in close enough to take the ground, we failed to find it. We drew off a little and anchored in disgust.

The Yacht Club proved to be as elusive by daylight and the reason became clear when, having hailed a man in a dinghy, we learnt that we were not in Vigo Bay but in the next bay to the north. Still, in this delightful cruising ground we had a very pleasant sail round to Villa-garcia where, although it was a Sunday, we had the gaff repaired. Off Finisterre it broke again, but under trysail and headsails with a brave southerly wind we made good time across the bay until we ran into fog. Out of this a huge French battleship appeared and vanished like a wraith. While we were remarking this apparition the Scottish youth—his one active contribution to the voyage, for which I forgive him all—drew our attention to a pillar buoy on the port bow and breakers ahead. Having put *Mischief* about and brought the buoy on to the starboard hand we passed close enough to discover that it was the Ar Men buoy marking the reef of that suggestive name for which we had been confidently heading. This was the last of our misadventures. Two days later, on 5 November, we tied up at Lymington town quay where I was left alone to clear up the mess below and to lick my wounds.

CHAPTER II

A REAL START

A man in a jail has more room, better food,
and commonly better company.

SAMUEL JOHNSON

I N SPITE OF ALL THAT HAD BEEN DONE at Palma, *Mischief* still had some defects. No less than three new spars were needed—a gaff, topmast, and bowsprit. The last two, which had always been a bit shaky, were now condemned. But she was full of food and in all other respects ready and, like her owner, raring to go. So much time and money had already been spent that it seemed infinitely more painful to cut one's losses at once than to spend more in the hope of ultimately accomplishing so refreshing an adventure. Yet in the gloom of winter, when the making of these spars had been put in hand and when I myself went frequently to Lymington to work on her, I constantly wondered whether by the summer there would be a skipper to sail her or a crew to man her. The supply of 'rash, inconsiderate, fiery voluntaries' who knew anything of either sailing or climbing had apparently dried up. Perhaps it was that too many of them agreed with the well known description of life at sea quoted above. As for a skipper, although I had more confidence I had no wish to take the job on myself if I could find someone better qualified, someone whose sea experience was such that all qualms and arguments on the part of the crew would have to be kept to themselves; and apart from the voyage out and back I had to have an experienced man to take charge when the shore party had landed.

When I got in touch with W. A. Procter, the man whom I had so luckily heard of at Oporto, I found him eager to make a long voyage and not a whit perturbed either by the proposed cruising ground or the prospect of a year's absence. Nor did he waver, as several others did, from his first decision. Having for several years owned a Falmouth quay punt he knew more about boats than I would ever hope to, though that is not extravagant praise. He was a retired civil servant and when I visited him and found to my alarm that he had a wife and three children I felt like a wrecker of homes. But Mrs Procter took a sensible view of what must have seemed a fairly wild scheme and, putting her husband's interests before her own, decided that a sea voyage would do him good and promised to wish us both God-speed when the time came. The only stipulation was that I should bring him back.

Having now at least the nucleus of a crew I began canvassing the services and the universities for young sailors and or climbers, inserting advertisements in the yachting press, and generally making my wants known as widely as I could. All came to nothing. Of two naval officers who would have liked to have come, one could not get leave, while the other could have leave but no pay. Some half-dozen undergraduates at different times volunteered and were accepted, only to withdraw later, deterred either by the advice of illiberal tutors or nervous parents. Of the twenty or so who answered the advertise-ment only two seemed worth interviewing. In the event one wanted to be paid and the other was looking for a passage to Canada. For the rest there were several girls and one married couple (an application which made me wince) while the others faded away after being told what was in store.

In the meantime, hoping much, as always, from time and chance, I went down to Lymington to work on the boat. Scrubbing out lock-ers and painting the inside; new ratlines had to be fitted to the shrouds ('rattling down' as an old shellback would say); a new net was needed under the bowsprit, while all the blocks had to be stripped down and greased and new strops fitted. The old barrel winch, which must have been born with the ship and which one felt should be turned by cap-stan bars, was replaced with a very good winch which I bought cheap in a scrap yard. To complete the luxury below, pumps were fitted so that the galley sink and wash-hand basin could be emptied without the necessity of anyone going on deck. The manager of the yard, a man built on generous lines and accustomed to jumping on board from the jetty a few feet above, noted with misgiving that the deck yielded under this treatment like a too-well-sprung dance floor. Shaking his head ominously he alarmed me by suggesting that a new deck might be a good thing, rightly pointing out that his weight was nothing to that of a South Atlantic comber. But Humphrey Barton who knew the ship by now reassured me and we compromised by putting supporting posts under the deck beams. Two of these also served the useful purpose of securing the main water tank (100 gal.) which previously had only been screwed to the cabin deck!

At this stage the means occupied so much of my time and attention that I was in danger of losing sight of the end. What should have been the simple, straightforward job of fitting out and manning a boat to go to South America had become so beset with unknown factors that it was difficult to make any firm plans for the more exacting part and object of the whole exercise, the work on the ice-cap. Ideally one would have wished, having crossed the ice-cap, to wander overland to Punta Arenas to rejoin the ship there; or better still to cross back by another route and be picked up at a fresh rendezvous. But how strong would the shore party be, would it include a scientist, and would there be anyone left in the ship upon whom one could rely to take her safely back to Punta Arenas? When discussing plans with the skipper in 1954 we had decided that the picking up of the shore party at any other place than that at which they had landed would be too hazardous, and that the best place to land would be at some spot in Peel Inlet, a long fjord running inland from the main channel some 300 miles distant from Punta Arenas.

Westward of Tierra del Fuego and stretching along the western coast of Patagonia for eleven degrees northwards from the Magellan Straits is a chain of islands known as the Patagonian Archipelago. In the *South America Pilot* this region is described as 'about as inhospitable a land as is to be found in the globe. The land is mountainous presenting an alternation of matted forest, bare rock, and deep bogs, and is intersected by many deep channels into peninsulas and islands as yet very imperfectly known. The scenery is magnificently stern; cloud and mist usually screen the higher peaks and snow fields'. Between these islands and the mainland are good navigable channels which afford a smooth water route of over 300 miles. By using these channels ships can avoid the heavy seas and tempestuous weather usually encountered when passing into the Pacific from the Magellan Straits.

Nowadays it is the usual route for traffic between Argentine and Chilean ports. These channels are lit at difficult or dangerous points by buoys or unmanned lights; at the southern and northern entrances there are two manned lighthouses. The channels and their numerous anchorages are well charted but from the main channel a number of fjords or inlets run eastwards for thirty to forty miles. These are not charted. They are named and that is all; for no one uses them except a few Canoe Indians and the occasional hunter of sea otters.

These inlets provide the only access to the glaciers and the glaciers are the only access to the ice-cap. We had to decide which of the many was the best. The inlets are not shown at all on the Admiralty charts, which are concerned only with the main channels, but by then I had got hold of a very useful series of maps. After the war, at the request of the Chilean government, the American Air Force had surveyed the whole of that difficult region from the outer islands fronting the Pacific eastwards to the Argentine lakes. It must have been a long, difficult, and hazardous task because the number of days on which a camera could be used are few, the weather is normally bad, and there are no emergency landing strips. The resulting maps had been printed on a 1:250,000 scale and as well as giving a good picture of the ice, showing which glaciers actually reached the sea, they give an accurate outline of the coasts of these inlets. They do not, of course, show any soundings. From these maps we had picked upon Peel Inlet as the most likely for our purpose. It penetrated furthest east so that the ice-cap crossing would be the shorter, and it contained no less than ten glaciers which reached the water as well as several others which came within a mile of the shore. Above all, close to the entrance to Peel Inlet from the main channel, there was a safe anchorage at a place called Puerto Bueno. Thus it seemed best to base ourselves on Puerto Bueno and to effect our landing in Peel Inlet. This inlet had been first visited in 1908 by the Chilean navy store ship *Meteoro* which spent a night there while the Swedish scientific party which it was carrying landed to geologise. Later in 1930 Michael Mason, the well-known writer, traveller, and yachtsman, visited it in *Violeta* a 15-ton steam launch which he had chartered at Punta Arenas. Thus we were not working altogether in the dark. The two books describing these two visits had an honoured place on *Mischief*'s bookshelf.

The adventure of crossing an ocean, the seeing of new lands and little-known coasts, and the setting foot on hitherto unvisited glaciers were for me sufficient reasons for travelling so far afield. But in these unromantic days the excuse of mere adventure is not enough. The path of the traveller is made smoother and the official wheels, which sooner or later have to be turned, turn more freely if he or one of his party purpose suffering in the cause of science. Indeed, one is hardly expected to travel—I use the word in the strict sense—for any other reason, and I found that almost the first questions asked by foreign journalists were about our scientific aims. One cannot provide for a yacht and a crew of five in South American ports on a travel allowance of £100 and so when applying for more money to the Bank of England—on the whole a serious-minded body—it would not do to offer a frivolous reason. Apart from the collecting of plants which I proposed to undertake I hoped to include in the shore party a geologist or glaciologist. It was unlikely he would be willing or able to waste four months at sea but I hoped that he could join us at Punta Arenas and then leave as soon as we got back. I have found by experience that the field geologist, the man who plies his hammer in the secret places of the earth, is not a common bird, while the glaciologist is rare indeed. For many years past young geologists who wish to get experience in the field have confined their activities to Spitsbergen and North East Land, a region which surely by now must be in fragments. For the 1954 attempt I had found a young Oxford geologist who was able to come and eager to do some glaciological work as well. He was to join us at Punta Arenas and the Everest Foundation were to contribute towards his passage. Even after the fiasco of that year he agreed to hold himself in readiness for the winter of 1955-56, but within a month of our departure he had the offer of a Fellowship and naturally took it.

In May 1955 affairs looked far from promising. There was a crew of one, no scientist, not even a mountaineer for the shore party. Suddenly things took a turn for the better. Through the Royal Artillery Yacht Club I got in touch with Lieut. M. R. Grove (he got his captaincy while we were in the Pacific) who, with the enterprise expected of gunner subalterns, volunteered to come. We met at Bala, halfway between Barmouth and Oswestry where he was stationed, with the result that he applied for a year's leave. Early in June this was granted—without pay, of course, but with the threat, too, that the lost year would not count for promotion. Over this hard condition the Treasury, with the help of the President of the Royal Geographical Society (himself a gunner), was later persuaded to relent. Michael Grove had had some slight experience of sailing and ahead of him lay ample time to gain more. He would gladly have made one of the shore party, which at this time consisted of only myself, but he had had no experience of climbing and once we had landed in Peel Inlet we would not have the time to train him. At Punta Arenas, when we were still short of the essential third man, I prepared for the worst by getting him a pair of climbing boots. However, he was never called upon to use them.

On the constantly changing list of possible or probable candidates, which for the last few months had kept me on tenterhooks, the name of Major E. H. Marriott, also a gunner, a member of the Alpine Club and an experienced climber, had frequently bobbed up. Having recently joined a party who were to sail a boat to New Zealand, and paying for the privilege, he had been finally struck off. It now seemed that after a difference of opinion with the skipper and owner he was again at a loose end. Charles Marriott, so called because his initials are E. H., had before the war sailed as far as the Canaries on a similar voyage before leaving the ship in much the same circumstances. But differences of opinion and jarring temperaments, leading often to the dispersal of crews and the abrupt ending of promising ventures, are common form in small boats, an occupational risk which cannot be insured against and which one must accept. The only long voyages free from crew trouble are usually made by man and wife—of which there are several recent examples—or by single-handers. So Charles Marriott was invited to join. As neither he nor Michael Grove was available before the first week of July I arranged to pick them up at Falmouth whence we would make our final departure.

Procter joined me at Lymington in mid-June, sailing day being tentatively fixed for the 24th. We had intended putting the boat on the hard at Falmouth in order to apply between tides a final coat of anti-fouling; but now we decided to have her slipped at Lymington, where she had been lying in a mud berth, so that we could have a look at the hull as well as give it proper time to dry before applying the paint. Meantime there were only the two of us to sail her to Falmouth. In the days when *Mischief* was a working boat and sailors were real sailors, the Pilot cutters were normally manned by two hands—occasionally, I believe, by one. In that delightful book *Messing about in Boats** there is a description of how the dinghy was got on board by the lone hand, by the bold but simple expedient of making the painter fast to the boom at the right place, letting the main sheet out, and then gybing the boom over, whereupon the dinghy sprang on board through an opening cut in the bulwarks while the hand leapt from the tiller to catch it by the stern and secure it. I did not see either Procter or myself attempting such a feat or even taking her quietly round to Falmouth by ourselves. We needed help and help was forthcoming.

An acquaintance of Procter's, near Petersfield, having heard of our project became eager to join in. This was John Van Tromp and I hoped he would have some of the qualities of his great namesake. He ran a small dairy farm. One hears of sailors swallowing the anchor and buying a farm but less often does one hear of anyone selling a farm in order to go to sea. Van Tromp, when he came down to Lymington to press his claim, startled me a little by his deerstalker hat. His claim, however, was one which appealed strongly to me for he volunteered to do all the cooking. On my list there were still the names of one or two waverers who had yet to make their decision and here was a man who had no doubts and who was ready to tackle the least pleasant job. As I was soon to learn, I am not alone in liking good food and plenty of it supplied at regular and not too infrequent intervals. But when a crew takes it in turn to cook this desirable end is seldom attained. On dry land or on calm days at sea cooking can be an agreeable pursuit, taxing and stimulating the imagination and occasioning many surprises; but *Mischief*'s galley is not ideally placed. It is in the fore part of the ship, between cabin and forepeak, where the motion is most lively. And when she is sailing on the wind the fore hatch, the main source of ventilation for the galley, must be kept closed. 'When they bring you a heifer be ready with the rope'. I therefore closed promptly with this welcome offer and John agreed to be with us on sailing day, bringing with him a friend called Tony who wanted to come as far as Falmouth. Tony, who had never been to sea,

---

*   By Surgeon Rear Admiral John R. Muir, Blackie 1938—*Ed*

had a bent for machinery and I unashamedly meant to use it to get out of Lymington river.

On 27 June, the last coat of anti-fouling having been put on, *Mischief* took the water. The engine did not start immediately, but it did as soon as we had turned on the petrol. Unobtrusively we stole away down the river, remarked only by some vigilant friends at the Yacht Club who gave us a one-gun salute which we acknowledged by dipping our colours. The three days down Channel proved uneventful except for the deathly sickness of John's friend, the anxious passage by night through a fleet of drifters, and the mistaking of Gribbin Head for Dodman Point by Procter who, as a Cornishman, should have known better.

At Falmouth we still had much to do. The bolster which supports the starboard shrouds had broken and had to be replaced, a job which the local yard did quickly and efficiently. Half a ton of stores sent down from Liverpool had to be put on board and stowed, formalities for taking on a small quantity of bonded stores observed, and water, petrol, and paraffin tanks refilled. In addition, a large air bubble in the compass indicated a leaking seal; we wanted a day's sailing to try the twin staysails; and another day to go to Newlyn to buy some composite rope. This is a six-strand rope of forty-two wires, each strand consisting of seven wires contained in a manila sheath. It is very strong, neither stretches nor swells, is impervious to chafe, and is the devil to coil. On a long voyage, especially in a gaff-rigged ship like *Mischief*, chafe is the great bugbear, the throat and peak halyards being most susceptible. When the original halyards showed signs of wear we reeved this composite rope and forgot about it.

To those who have to do with them, ships seem to lend a sense of purpose and of service. The compass adjuster might have been a high priest of a religion called terrestrial magnetism who regarded compasses as sentient beings, of more account than the ships and men they guided, and fully responsible for their behaviour. He looked at our compass disapprovingly, shook it, turned it round once or twice, and advised me to drop it overboard. If I insisted he would gladly remove the air bubble without charge, but the compass was old and its period of recovery after deflection so prolonged that it was no longer trustworthy. In defence of an old friend I pointed out that this despised instrument had brought us safely home from the Mediterranean (omitting the story of that horrible apparition the Ar Men buoy), whereupon he merely remarked on the wonderful ways of Providence. In the end I took his advice.

The day allotted for trying out the twin staysails turned out wet, windy, and rough. Tony came with us and enjoyed it but a girl friend of Van Tromp's who came for the sail did not. The mainsail had to come down, never an easy job in a strong wind, before the staysail booms were fitted to the mast, one with a jaw and the other with a gooseneck which dropped into the spider band on the mast. When they were up the twins pulled like mad and we were confident that with some adjustments, particularly to the mast fitting, they would be powerful aids to trade wind sailing. Once more under the mainsail we turned and scuttled back to Falmouth.

The time had come for Michael Grove and Charles Marriott to show up. Every time we rowed ashore we scanned the pier until at last I descried a bearded figure in a white yachting cap who, viewed from far enough off to conceal the slightly moth-eaten blazer and flannel trousers, had something of the air of King Edward waiting to join the royal cutter *Britannia*. It was Charles Marriott whom we gladly took off, for his appearance did *Mischief* credit. Michael Grove soon followed and on the morning of 6 July we went ashore for the last time to lay in fresh food. At 10 a.m. we got our anchor and sailed out, and very few of those who watched us go knew whither we were bound. 'It is not the beginning but the continuing of the same until it be thoroughly finished that yieldeth the true glory.'

CHAPTER III

THE FIRST LEG

Where lies the land to which the ship would go
Far, far ahead, is all her seamen know

CLOUGH

A LTHOUGH IT SMACKS of seamanlike efficiency, to say that we got
our anchor and sailed out is not strictly accurate. It leaves much
unsaid. In fact we had two anchors down and their cables were so lov-
ingly entwined that for some time the foredeck was the scene of a fearful struggle and resounded with unseamanlike oaths. We passed Black
Rock, and the sentiments appropriate to watching from the deck of
a small ship, outward bound on a long voyage, the receding shores
of one's native land, had barely found expression when the shores
ceased to recede. The wind which had hitherto been light now failed
altogether and for two hours we drifted off the headland of St Anthony
viewing its not remarkable features from many different angles.

After lunching on deck, for it was a warm day for England, we
got a breeze from the south-west, hoisted the Genoa and streamed the
log in the hope that the voyage had really begun. By evening we had
caught many mackerel. To add to our pleasure the wind went round to
north-west so that we were able to lay the course for Ushant; or rather
15 miles west of Ushant, for after our experience the previous year I
intended giving that noted sea-mark a wide berth. Our next port of
call was Las Palmas in the Canaries. Except for the purpose of check-
ing our untried navigation the sighting of any land on the way would
have been unnecessary. It is 1500 odd miles to Las Palmas which we
reckoned upon reaching inside three weeks.

With four of us available for watch-keeping—the cook very properly being exempt—we had an easy time. The day from 8 a.m. to 8
p.m. was divided into three watches of four hours each and the night
into four watches of three hours each. Thus, without recourse to dog

36

watches, one's watch changed automatically, and on every fourth day a man had practically the whole day off or the whole night in. In order to make life still easier, when sails had to be shifted we did it if possible at the change of watch. At nightfall we tried by shortening sail to ensure that the watch below was not disturbed. Naturally this did not always happen. A peaceful sky and a steady barometer might belie their promise, wind and weather might change without warning, so that that which might have been done in daylight and at leisure, had to be done in darkness, in a hurry, by men half asleep. More often a disturbed night was our own fault. Because of a natural dislike of slowing the ship when she was reeling off the miles it was too easy to leave our light sails up or the mainsail unreefed, to trust to careless hope and to use reason to thrust aside what we did not fancy.

According to the late Conor O'Brien, a complicated rig on an ocean-going yacht justifies itself in giving the crew something to do. Other than watch-keeping and sail-changing there is not much for the crew of a well-found ship on a long voyage under normal conditions to do, for the sail changing has neither the frequency nor the urgency that obtains in ocean racing. Naturally one tries to get the best one can out of the boat, but the comfort of the crew, the safety of the gear and the wear and tear upon it, are vastly more important than speed. The crew has to carry on for weeks or months and there is a limit to the amount of spare gear that can be carried or to the repairs that can be affected in mid-ocean.

Even so life was too hard for some of the crew, who during their trick at the helm needed cushions to support their body, an awning to cover their head, and a book to distract their mind. But at least one of us, John Van Tromp, had no sinecure. Those who invoke hunters, sharks, wolves, hyenas, or cormorants as examples of voracity have much to learn. Procter, and Michael Grove, too, when he had found his sea legs, could eat their way past any of these with hardly a pause for breath. And since neither Charles Marriott nor I would be described as delicate feeders the cook had his hands full in preparing meals and clearing up. In addition, by inclination and because he had more knowledge of it than the rest of us, John attended to the engine when needed and looked after the little charging engine. He also did any electrical repairs. They were often needed as the wiring throughout the

ship was amateurish and the fittings not so waterproof as they should
have been. He spent his spare time fishing and perhaps once in a thousand miles or so throughout the voyage his efforts were rewarded by a
big fish. Those were red-letter days.

Procter was a good carpenter and handyman so that any such
work fell to him, while I looked after the rigging. As I have said the
amount of wear and tear that goes on at sea sailing night and day,
particularly at night when sheets are eased or shortened and the necessary shifting of the anti-chafe material ('scotsmen') is overlooked, is
a never-ending source of worry. There are few days when there is not
any stitching of sails or splicing of rope and wire to be done. There can
be no one who goes to sea for fun who takes no interest in the behaviour of the ship, the set of the sails, the ever changing pattern of sea
and sky, the sea birds which are seldom absent and the fish which, we
found, were so seldom present. As long as the ship is moving, prefera-
bly in the right direction, one is seldom bored even in the most lifeless
ocean and interest is quickly restored by the mere sight of another ship
or other sign of life. Only in very light airs or flat calms, when there is
no progress and there is nothing to be done or to be seen, is boredom
felt, and the effect of such times upon the temper and morale of the
crew is very obvious.

Our first night at sea passed peacefully for all except Mike Grove
who mistook the rising moon for a sail approaching at speed, shone
the torch on our sails, and was on the point of rousing me out. Next
day when the wind had freshened from east-north-east we gybed over
to the port tack and logged what proved to be our best run for many
a long day, 140 miles. How thankful we were for a wind which gave us
such a flying start and for a sea which as yet exacted no tribute. The
subsequent shortening of sail by taking two rolls in the mainsail and
handing the big Genoa served to mark our apprehensions rather than
worsening weather; for in the early days we seldom failed to expect the
worst, seeing menace in every cloud and a gale in every gust. But by
the time we were well into the Bay of Biscay three of us who had not
yet found our sea legs were in poor shape. The fair wind took us with a
lessening speed right across the Bay and early on the fourth morning,
with the wind falling light, we sighted land. During this run three of
us had been busily taking sights, more by way of practice than in the

expectation of getting trustworthy results. Before setting a course for the Canaries we had intended taking our departure from Cape Finisterre and to make sure of not missing it we had steered a little to the east. The land ahead was undoubtedly the north coast of Spain, somewhere, we thought, in the neighbourhood of Coruña. With the aid of binoculars, the hand-bearing compass, and the appropriate 'Pilot', we speedily identified the Tower of Hercules, a square dark tower at the western entrance of Coruña Bay. Procter, who two months before had been there in my old acquaintance *Iyruna* on her way home from Oporto, recognised it, and the adjacent features seemed to fit. After one wrong assumption it is remarkable how easily the neighbouring marks on a coast line can be made to conform and how long it is before discrepancies become so glaring that the original assumption has to be abandoned. Prominent buildings noted in the 'Pilot' are cheerfully allowed to have been knocked down or put up since that invaluable guide was written; woods to have been planted or felled; and awkward hills which refuse to fit into the picture are either ignored or assumed to have been swallowed by an earthquake. Until at last common sense prevails and one is obliged sadly to admit that nothing fits and that one is looking at an entirely different piece of coast. We were all adrift. We were off Cape Ortegal, and in the evening, after we had sailed in desultory fashion some twenty miles along the coast, the Tower of Hercules was unmistakably identified by its light.

That we were out in our reckoning and had made a bad landfall was attributed to our being set in by the tide. The navigator can always attribute his errors—unless, of course, they are fatal—to abnormal tidal sets or the perverse behaviour of currents, whereas the man who leads his party into the wrong valley or on to the wrong ridge has no such scapegoat and is written down an ass. We should have to do better after taking our departure for the Canaries, for it would not do to miss them. We had two sextants, both, judging by their venerable appearance, immediate successors of the astrolabe. Both had Vernier scales, which are less easy to read than micrometers, and unless one had a fearful squint Procter's sextant was very difficult to read. Moreover, it was useless for taking star sights unless one discarded the telescope. But for £5, which was all it cost, one can't expect refinements, and it gave reliable results.

For working sights Procter used the popular Air Navigation Tables. One objection to them is that for a long voyage a great many massive volumes must be carried; for instance, for a voyage like that which Conor O'Brien made, twenty volumes would be needed. The objection I had to them was that until the answer had been plotted on the chart it did not mean anything. Following the example of the 'Master' I used the tables published by the U.S. Hydrographic Office, H.O. 211, a slim volume of fifty pages. With this and a Nautical Almanac one could circumnavigate the globe. Using these, in less than five minutes one knew without plotting the distance and direction of the ship's line of position from the dead reckoning position. Charles, who in pre-war days had studied celestial navigation at what he called the Military College of Nonsense, was our acknowledged expert, at any rate, in the theory of the subject. But he had refused to move with the times. He preferred time-honoured methods employing logarithms, haversines, cosecants, and God knows what, and these seemed not only to take longer than ours but gave more scope for human fallibility. The scope, in fact, was so wide that an error of a degree or so in working became known to us as a 'Charles'. On the other hand a good intercept or, if we were working several star sights, a small 'cocked hat', was called a 'Henry' in honour of the great Navigator. Sometimes when three or even four or five were taking sights it became a little difficult to reconcile the results or even to pick one's way through the spider's web which soon adorned the chart. But I had the last word, and by a combination of the theory of probabilities, a knowledge of the instruments used, and of those who used them, I decided which to accept and which to reject and plotted our position accordingly. It sounds haphazard. A court of inquiry, had we ever had to face one, might have taxed us with awkward questions, but such problems kept everyone's interest alive and before we were through we were at least competent.

The wind falling light obliged us to motor until we were far enough round the corner of Spain to lay the course for Las Palmas. We did not see Finisterre but on 12 July took our departure from Cape Torinana about ten miles north of it. A day later we picked up the Portuguese Trades, the northerly winds which had so plagued us the previous autumn and which now gave us runs of over a hundred miles a day. As we were running before the wind it did not seem so fresh as I remembered, but the crew of a 14-ton sloop, the *Maid of Pligh*, which was beating to windward homeward bound, probably thought it quite fresh enough. We waved heartily and that was all. In the old days when sailing ships met at sea they would often heave to for a yarn, a pleasant custom that we might well have followed; but we suffered from the universal complaint of being in a hurry, with no time to stand and stare, let alone exchange news with a fellow voyager.

The same night, for a different reason, we not only failed to exchange news but even to exchange names. Shortly after midnight in my watch we sailed close to a large, brilliantly lit passenger liner lying stationary, with two red lights hoisted to show she was not under command. After opening communication with the Aldis lamp and giving our name we found ourselves unable to read morse well enough to learn her name or why she lay there, a failure the more disgraceful since we had on board one serving gunner officer and two veterans. That a yacht should carry a signalling lamp and only be able to use it for the highly improper purpose of scaring steamers ('steamer-scarer' is the yachtsman's name for his lamp) is, to say the least, unseamanlike.

A similar thing had happened the previous year in the same waters in daylight when we encountered the *Roxburgh Castle*. The R.A.S.C. corporal knew morse, or thought he did, and when asking for our position got on swimmingly until they began sending the latitude and longitude. The figures baffled him. In spite of repetitions he could make nothing of them, so that finally she circled slowly round us—they could almost have shouted to us—making hoists of flags until they were sure we had understood. Just because we could not read morse she had been delayed half an hour. Though one may send morse with great satisfaction to oneself it does not follow that it is always read if one is sending from a yacht. If there is anything of a sea running half the letters spelt out may be obscured by waves. We therefore painted our name in large letters on the dinghy cover. If we thought a ship was going to pass close to us, and sometimes they did alter course in order to do so, we lashed this to the rail, hoisted our ensign, and thus satisfied their curiosity and concealed our signalling inability.

It is astonishing how quickly a southward bound yacht, even though it is not a flyer, reaches the warmer weather for which the crew long. Sweaters and shirts are shed, shorts and bathing bags appear, and the sun-starved northerner's passion for getting his body well tanned by the sun is given full rein. But perfect comfort must not be expected by folks who go a-pleasuring. After a few more degrees of southing the sun-worshippers are wearing dark glasses, rigging awnings over the cockpit, and taking refuge in the shade of the cabin where they do nothing but complain of the heat.

When we had outrun the Portuguese trades a westerly wind carried us along until in about lat. 35° we were caught up in the strong embrace of the true north-east trades. With a wind which never fell below force 4 (about 16 knots) and more often reached force 5 or 6 sailing was exhilarating. We lowered the mainsail and stowed the boom, hoisted the twin staysails and let her go. The sky overhead with little fleecy clouds sailing across was a pale reflection of the sparkling blue sea flecked with foam and dancing spray. Rolling became continuous and sometimes heavy as the pursuing waves surged by, lifting the counter with a friendly shove forwards and slightly sideways, before hissing past the rail and depositing a dollop of water on deck by way of salute. Steering was easy, for there was no fear of a gybe. Sheets had scarcely to be touched, and perhaps best of all with this rig the gear subject to chafe was reduced to a minimum. *Mischief* seemed to enjoy sailing before a wind that blew true and steady as the wind of a bellows, as much as did her crew. She frequently showed her pleasure by some very lively rolling. This rhythmic rolling, inseparable from downwind sailing, becomes a nuisance, particularly at meal times, when a man needs two pair of hands, or when any work has to be done on deck. Every few minutes the ship would glide gently into what would become a crescendo of rolling, each successive roll becoming livelier and longer until the dislodging of the helmsman from his seat or a loud crash from the galley, announced that she had had her bit of fun. Then she would sail demurely along until tempted by the laughing waves to do it again. One could amost hear her humming to herself:

> Roll me over, in the clover,
> Roll me over, lay me down, and do it again.

With the coming of the trades we began to see flying fish in abundance and sometimes we got a few on board. For this effortless form of fishing neither patience nor implements are needed, only rough weather. After a night of heavy rolling a search of the scuppers and under the dinghy at times provided enough fish for breakfast. Another welcome visitor was a little brown and white striped pilot fish which perhaps mistook us for the shark he usually attends. He took station a foot or two ahead of *Mischief*'s rushing forefoot and swam there tirelessly for something like 300 miles. Perhaps fish sleep while swimming, as do horses when standing up, but this little chap seemed neither to sleep nor eat food. We watched him carefully, noting in the log at every change of watch whether Fidelio, as we called him was present and correct. We missed him sorely when he left us as he did the night before we sighted the Islands.

We are never satisfied with the present. Change is what we really like and if there is too much of that we begin to long for stability. Content though *Mischief*'s crew were with life at sea we eagerly awaited the approach of land, although I for one knew that making port would inevitably give me work and worry. After only sixteen days at sea we looked forward with mounting excitement to our first port of call. What sort of landfall would we make? Or again, would there be any land to see? Grand Canary, on which is Las Palmas, lies between the islands of Teneriffe and Fuerteventura and is separated from them by channels thirty and forty-five miles wide respectively. By making a bad shot either way, and attended by the mischance of thick weather, the unskilful mariner could easily whistle through either channel in a matter of hours and not see land at all. In clear weather the veriest duffer should be able to make his landfall, since the Peak of Teneriffe (12,140 ft.) can be seen from seventy miles and the other islands have their own mountains.

By the morning of 22 July we had run our distance and in spite of a smoky haze we fully expected to see the Peak towering above it. No such welcome sight appeared. Only the passing of three or four steamers showed we were on course and probably nearing a port. Visibility became worse. We were sailing fast in rough water and we had to decide whether to run off westwards where we thought Grand Canary should be or to carry on and hope to see land later when the sun burnt up the haze. In the skipper's opinion, though it would not have been helpful to express it:

Beyond the clouds, beyond the waves that roar,
There may indeed, or may not be, a shore.

We raced on until about 10.30 a.m. The weather was as thick as ever and as the fear of having overshot our mark had become unbearable we handed the twins and hove to under reefed main and reefed stay-sail, for it was now blowing hard. Thus we lay until about noon when Charles, who is gifted with remarkably keen eyesight, cheered us with a cry of 'Land'. Sure enough to the north-west a blurred shape showed darkly through the haze. We let draw and sailed towards it when it presently resolved itself into Punta Gando, the easternmost point of Grand Canary some ten miles south of Las Palmas.

Our landfall had been good enough. Had we but had faith in our reckoning and turned west at 8 a.m. we should have sighted the town. As we were now near the south end of the island I suggested sailing round and up the west coast in the lee of the land. This was vetoed on the grounds that we should have a hard job weathering the north end, so we put about and began the long beat back. Weary work it was. It took us the best part of twenty-four hours to make good the ground lost in two hours, but early on the afternoon of the 23rd we dropped anchor off the Las Palmas Yacht Club. Domingo, a man who speaks English and is well known to visiting yachts, came off. He startled me by insisting that if we thought of going ashore all together we must employ a watchman, otherwise water-thieves, bold as brass and cunning as monkeys, would strip the ship to the last nut and bolt. One yacht, we were told, had had her entire lead keel removed. Having thus prepared his listeners for bad tidings Domingo added that the watchman's fee would be 15s. a night. I agreed to this blackmail, if blackmail it was, rather than abide the consequences of refusal. So Johnnie the watchman was installed that night and proved a good investment. He rowed us back to the ship at all hours of the night as well as rendering us many other services. Domingo acted his self-assumed part of ship's agent well, saw that we were not cheated too much, and was very grateful for what we gave him.

CHAPTER IV

THE LONG HAUL

And where the land she travels from? Away,
Far, far behind, is all that they can say.

CLOUGH

U NLIKE OUR VISITS to South American ports, in Las Palmas we
did not make any friends. But it was from the points of view
of climate and amenities the most pleasant. When I say Las Palmas,
I mean in fact Puerto de la Luz, the port four miles distant from
the city. Here food is as cheap again as in its smarter neighbour,
while on the wide esplanade fronting the harbour are places shaded
by trees and sheltered by trellises where one can sit and drink
and watch the world go by. In the few South American ports we
entered, neither the climate nor the streets make any provision for
such alfresco idling—in my opinion the best attraction a town can
offer.

Visiting yachts are common at Las Palmas, for most yachts bound
for the West Indies or America call there; nevertheless, we attracted
some attention and were perhaps not altogether unworthy of it. By
now Michael had a beard the colour of Yorkshire parkin, shaped
like a horse collar, which put me in mind of Facey Romford as por-
trayed by Leech. While it was worth anybody's money to see Charles,
bearded like a minor prophet and still crowned with his yachting cap,
strolling along with Van Tromp in his deerstalker hat. Nor were we the
only strange types loose in Las Palmas. There was the ex-5th engineer
who had saved money while working in some desert on oil installa-
tions and was spending it in the Canaries living in a cave with a milk-
maid. And there was the ex-Indian Army officer who was extremely
correct, but who ate with us at our restaurant in shirt sleeves and
braces—on the same principle, one supposes, that if you find your-
self among swine it is best to dispense with a plate. On shore, except

for the occasional rendezvous at this restaurant, the crew having seen enough of each other at sea, parted company. Michael, while showing a remarkable facility for penetrating almost upon arrival the more select social circles, made a business of collecting all sorts of information dealing with local political and economic affairs. Procter, a classical scholar who spoke Spanish more grammatically, I was told, than a Spaniard, usually seemed to find his way into the family of some earnest student who wished to practise his English. 'When you enter a byre, low; when you enter a pen, bleat,' is a sound maxim, but Procter sometimes carried his affability so far—that is, when on shore—as to lead to embarrassment. Visitors having been warmly invited would arrive on board at the most inconvenient times; or I would return to find the cabin full to overflowing, a painstakingly strident lesson in English in progress over the table, and I would have to take refuge on shore. Both he and Michael were ardent sightseers and made a tour of the island. As we discovered later, however, it was Charles who was the real dyed-in-the-wool tourist. But Las Palmas was to him familiar ground as he had been dumped here on his first deep-sea voyage after a quarrel with the owner of the yacht. Having no money to speak of, he had lived for a fortnight on bananas and had not yet got over it. This time it was John Van Tromp who had no money, there being some hitch over the sale of his farm, so that he was compelled to live like a recluse—though not on a banana diet. While I, besides having much to do, never have difficulty in suppressing any momentary hankering after social gaiety.

As we arrived on a Saturday and were hoping to leave the following Friday, we had only four working days available to us. At Falmouth we had had made a collar fitting to the mast about five feet above the deck to take the inboard end of the staysail booms. At least that was the height I liked it to be, but Procter, who is tall, always tried to fix it a couple of feet higher, ostensibly on the grounds that there was more wind up there but in fact to avoid cracking his head on the boom. We had been advised by experts to mount these booms forward of the mast, so now we employed a blacksmith to make an iron fitting which could be bolted to the bitts. At the same time we got him to make a harpoon, so that when fishing we could if we wished transfer the initiative from the fish to ourselves. In a strong wind this new iron fitting proved to be too flimsy. Within five minutes of the twins being hoisted the strain bent it and the bitts themselves shook visibly.

Taking petrol aboard occupied most of a day and involved a cart and horse to fetch the 40-gal. drum, and Domingo's dinghy, a much stouter one than ours, to bring it off. Even so we came within an ace of sinking the dinghy and losing the drum, although when we were discussing the threatened calamity, Charles, after doing in his head a complicated sum, assured us that at least the drum would float. On the last day we took in fresh stores: bread of a particular size, specially baked, and guaranteed to keep for three weeks; potatoes, the best we ever had (they were in perfect condition nine weeks later at Monte-video); carrots, sweet peppers, bags of onions which we ate both raw and cooked, and a hand of bananas; tomato paste, invaluable for *pasta sciutta* and *risotto*; and *chilli* paste, a species of bottled lightning for striking fire from dull dishes.

On Friday 29 July we motored round to the water-boat to fill our tanks. When her crew heard whither we were bound they showed their concern by urging us to fill every container we had, however small. This we did, and then like camels, took a last, long drink ourselves before water became precious. We reckoned that at worst the 4600 miles ahead of us would take eighty days, so that with 200 gal. we could use 2½ gal. a day. The responsibility for this was put firmly on John. Under his control we were not allowed to drink water except as tea or coffee at meal times and could use only an occasional half-mugful for shaving or tooth cleaning. Later, as it happened, we were able to refill one of our tanks with rain water, but we could have gone to Montevideo on our 200 gal. without inconvenience.

After settling accounts with Domingo and Johnnie we hoisted sail, cast off from the water-boat and began the long haul southwards. Leaving Las Palmas in a sailing ship bound south is as carefree as stepping on to a train. As soon as we were outside we hoisted the twins and metaphorically sat back. By 5 p.m. our old acquaintance Punta Gando was abeam. We streamed the log and managed to snarl it with the fishing line. It took us two hours to sort out the tangle. As fishermen we were always rich in hope if poor in possession. We usually had a line out, sometimes two, and if these were forgotten when going about or in moments of crisis, as they sometimes were, the consequent lash-up was deplorable.

Our next landfall, we hoped, would be St Vincent in the Cape Verde Islands some 900 miles to the south-west. Thence we would stand on to the southward without trying to make much westing, aiming at crossing the equator in about long. 29°W. This was the track used in other days by sailing ships bound round Cape Horn. Where possible we followed the track for sailing ships laid down on the *Ocean Pilot Charts* published by the U.S. Hydrographic Office. There is a chart for each ocean for each month of the year showing not only the recommended track for steam or sail, but also the prevalent winds and currents, the seasonal limits of the trades, percentages of gales and calms, sea temperatures, normal barometric pressures, and much else. These charts are based on observations and information collected by Lieutenant Maury (1806–73), an American naval officer who as a mid-shipman had spent four years on a cruise round the world. Having been put in charge of what later became the Hydrographic Office he devoted much of his time to establishing which were the best routes for sailing ships on all the standard voyages at any particular time of the year. He did this mainly by distributing specially prepared log books to masters of vessels and thus accumulating a mass of data. Without the information to be found on these charts or in the British Admiralty publication *Ocean Passages of the World*, which comprise the carefully sifted data of thousands of voyages, a sailing ship man would spend many more days at sea.

For the next seven days we ran in the full swing of the trades. These were days of glorious sailing. The sun blazed down till the pitch in the seams bubbled, the dazzling white twins swayed and curtsied until their booms kissed the water, while the ship rolled lazily along on her run of more than a hundred miles every day. All this happened with little or no exertion on our part. We even had flying fish for break-fast every morning with no exertion at all. But the Cape Verde Islands which we were rapidly approaching seem to upset the steadiness of the trades. The wind became fitful and one wondered whether or not the wind would be truer away to the west of the islands. But the idea of taking such a course would be rejected when one remembered what a fillip the interest and morale of the crew receives from the sight of land.

For me there is something about islands that rouses a more lively interest than a mere line of coast, an aura of romance such as is expressed in Flecker's:

A ship, an isle, and a sickle moon.

To sight one, even the smallest barren ash-heap, excites curiosity — whether or not there be a landing place, water, or even any life at all; and to be on one is to enjoy the delights of the sea without the disgusts.

Most of the Cape Verde Islands are ash-heaps, ash-heaps which with their warm colouring appear to be still smouldering. Early on 6 August we sighted the bold headland of Lombo de Boi, Bull Point, at the north-east end of Santo Antao. With light airs we sailed and drifted through the channel between it and St Vincent to the east, past the main harbour Porto Grande, remarking as we passed, the barracks, the prison, the hospital, all the tokens, in short, of civilization. We crept past the signal station on Ilheu dos Passeros dutifully making our number (the signal flags MKCP) and as usual evoking no response; for a yacht's signal flags are too small to be read at any distance. It is doubtful whether a set of flags is worth carrying. It was very hot and we had barely steerage way; so we ignored the warning given in the *Pilot* that sharks frequent the bay, dived overboard and swam about the ship.

The sun sank and the ruddy glow of the barren hills changed to violet and then to deep purple as we drifted along the rock coast towards Ponta Machado, the western extremity of the island. On this cape there is a lighthouse called Donna Amelia, a name which occasioned some chaff, mostly at Mike's expense, concerning the lighthouse keeper's daughter. About two in the morning I came on deck, perhaps by chance, perhaps because of that instinct which is supposed to rouse the sleeping mariner when his ship is in danger, but probably because Mike had called me to report the Amelia light abeam. Abeam with a vengeance. The thing was virtually above us. We were so close that I could have sworn I heard the light revolving and had the lighthouse keeper's daughter been on watch she could certainly have blown Mike kisses. Though the ship still had way she appeared to my shocked eyes to be getting sucked into a small bight beyond the headland where evidently—though the *Pilot* forbears to mention it—there lurked what that exemplary work sometimes refers to as a *bastardo*. With the help of the engine we won clear and I was thankful to see Amelia's baleful eye gradually recede and eventually disappear.

Having cleared the islands we had only one more good day of trade wind sailing before the wind failed, leaving us still two degrees north of its normal summer limit. The Doldrums, the belt of calms and rain squalls that lies between the north-east and south-east trade wind systems, is furthest north and at its widest in August when it covers about five degrees of latitude. These limits are, of course, only rough and may vary even from week to week. With luck a ship might be only three or four days in the Doldrums before picking up the trades on the other side, or she might remain more or less becalmed for a fortnight or more, fraying the tempers of her crew as well as the sheets, halyards, and sails. We had a weary time. Instead of handing the sails we left them up, the sheets hard in and the boom amidships, watching every catspaw that ruffled the oily sea in the hope that presently we might be able to let draw. On some days rain squalls burst frequently and with great violence, but if they brought any wind with them it might be from any direction. It was fun turning out naked in this heavy rain for a fresh water wash. We filled one of our 30-gal. tanks with great ease and had lots of water for washing clothes. On our shore-going clothes green mould sprouted freely. When it was not raining a clammy heat enveloped us. Buckets of sea water or a bathe overside brought some relief, but this resource was of little avail when the temperature of air and sea became the same, 80°F.

In the old days patience, a virtue very liable to be fatigued by exercise, was the only real remedy for this state of affairs. Other remedies were usually tried, such as whistling, throwing a pack of cards into the sea, or sticking a knife in the mast. But in order to be really effective the knife should be stuck in by a clergyman and seafaring clerics were not common. We ourselves were not free from these beliefs. When whistling failed we threw coins—Spanish pesetas of very nominal value—overboard on the quarter from which we wished the wind to come. But on the whole it is more effective to make use of an engine and petrol. By using these freely and by taking advantage of every puff of wind we worked our way steadily south, making good about forty miles a day. The longest continuous running of the engine was nine hours, and

The twin staysails boomed out from the mast; later both booms were
fitted to the one collar on the mast; the dinghy, usually full of sails,
was a favourite berth in calm weather

how grateful we were when we could shut it off. How we reviled the noise and the fumes in the cabin, and how we rejoiced in the succeeding stillness, with the musical ripple of water along the sides and the slat of the sails as they began to fill. Even with the help of the engine we endured eight days of these trying conditions until our boredom ended suddenly with a day of heavy rain, high wind, and steep seas. This violent but welcome change cost us the light Genoa. We had left it up too long and the clew blew out. When the following day dawned bright and clear we though we had at last escaped from the Doldrums but in fact four more days were to pass before we felt the first welcome breath of the south-east trades in about lat. 3°N.

But this baffling region is not without its interest. Marine life which hitherto had consisted mainly of flying fish and Portuguese men o'war (the nautilus with its delicate-coloured sail which abound in tropical and sub-tropical waters) became more varied. We thought it was about time. Accounts of voyages, all no doubt written by honourable men, in which bonito, albicore, dorado, and barracouta are seen or even caught on every other page, where the grim triangular fins of sharks ceaselessly circle the ship, and where whales rub their barnacles off on her bottom, had whetted our appetites and roused expectation to a height that was never to be realised. But on a day of oily calm, after a vast school of porpoises had played round for hours and finally taken themselves off, the helmsman did at last raise the cry of 'Shark'. So indiscriminating were we then that any large, unpleasing looking fish was labelled shark, and this may well have been one, for there are many kinds. He never surfaced but remained a few feet below and never far from our stern, a vague, green, disquieting shape. Horace, as we called him, was interested in food but in a languid sort of way. He followed us with some persistence for several days. Bathing stopped immediately, although I entered him in the log as merely a giant South Atlantic sea frog. Then Procter, the mildest of men, went berserk and harpooned an inoffensive dolphin gambolling round the forefoot. By the time we had it on board the harpoon was bent like a hoop. Some of us had an uneasy feeling that the consequences of such violence might rival those that befell the Ancient Mariner. Nevertheless, we ate him and for the first meal or two felt grateful. After that it palled, for the meat is like venison, dark and very rich. Soon after this we caught our first dorado (also called a dolphin). This was literally a very different kettle of fish, glorious to see and glorious to eat. He is anything up to 5ft. long, with a long fin running down his back, a Roman nose, and brilliant greeny-gold metallic hues which in the dying fish undergo quick changes. It is a fine thing to see him leaping ferociously after smaller fish, finer to see him on deck, and finest of all to have him on one's plate.

Quite apart from this choice of dark or white meat we lived well at this time. As an experiment I had brought a quantity of dehydrated food from the Ministry of Agriculture Experimental Factory, Aberdeen—minced beef, spinach, carrot, cabbage, and meat and vegetable blocks. All were so easily and quickly cooked and so excellent (the cabbage and carrot might have been straight from the garden) that I regretted having made the vulgar mistake of not taking enough. Even on hot mornings we fortified ourselves with porridge as belly-timber, and in the evening we turned hungrily upon large helpings of potatoes, rice or maccaroni in various guises, followed often by steamed puddings with which John had a happy knack. A little too much carbohydrate, perhaps, especially considering the heat, but we had no dietitian on board to point out that we were probably digging our graves with our teeth, and we thrived well enough. The puddings traced their origin back to an idle day off the Spanish coast when I made a cake. The recipe was no secret, so I handed it verbally to John who speedily discovered that 'Skipper's Mixture', as it was called, was equally adapted to baked cakes or steamed puddings. On Saturday evenings we had a drink, for not one of us was a rigid abstainer. Sunday was curry night. We felt obliged to limit this to one night a week on account of Michael whose appetite for curry was a little immoderate.

For some time now we had enjoyed the full glory of the southern sky at night—the Cross with its two pointers, Canopus, Fomalhaut, Achernar, Antares, and the two Magellanic Clouds glowing faintly and mysteriously like straying portions of the Milky Way. (These cloud-like clusters, though named after him, were known before Magellan's time.) Charles, whom we knew as the 'Astronomer Royal' and to whom we referred, as it were, for heavenly guidance, pointed out these and many lesser stars with curious names like Nunki, Shaula, and Kaus Australis. For sights we used the major stars and planets and left that temptingly easy target the moon for better men; for the working of her sights, with the numerous necessary corrections and the consequent increased opportunities for errors, generally gave startling results. In low latitudes there were few early mornings or late evenings when three or four suitable stars or planets could not be seen, but in higher latitudes we rarely got good star sights. In the North Atlantic there was usually cloud, poor horizons, or rough weather. If one quarter of the sky was clear, the horizon under it would be hazy, or clouds permitted such a fleeting glimpse of a star that even with the approximately correct angle on the sextant beforehand it could not be picked up, much less brought down to the horizon. Considering which exasperating circumstances, the navigator would exclaim against the Creator's arrangements in somewhat the same style as that credited to Lord Jeffrey: 'Damn the solar system. Bad light; planets too distant; pestered with comets; feeble contrivance; could make a better myself.'

On 29 August we crossed the equator in long. 28°W. and celebrated the event with a plum pudding. This was about the right place for a sailing ship bound for South America to cross the line. The south equatorial current sets west at the rate of about thirty miles a day and if a vessel bound south gets too far west there is some danger that she may not be able to weather Cape San Roque. A sailing vessel unlucky enough to be set to leeward of this cape would have to fetch a huge circuit of the North Atlantic before she could regain her proper course towards the equator for a second attempt. Although we were well placed we were being set west more than we liked and we could not steer south owing to the wind blowing persistently from that quarter rather than from the south-east as it should have done. The current, too, seemed to be working overtime. To go about on the other tack and sail away from the American coast demanded more strength of mind than we possessed, so we kept the ship close-hauled and our fingers crossed, praying for a wind that would let us sail a point free so that we should not be set down towards St Paul's Rocks or Fernando Noronha and eventually fail to weather San Roque.

In spite of the disturbing westerly set we could never be in danger of this, provided our sights were correct. We had long since ceased to get any time signals, but we knew the rate of the deck watch, we had not yet forgotten to wind it, and we felt that our reckoning could not be far out. On 2 September a noon sight showed us that we were on the same latitude as Fernando Noronha and still some ninety miles to the east of it. But as yet the south-east trades, which we had expected would blow bold and true like the north-east trades, were weak and variable. Still we were getting southwards all the time and were encouraged by the sight of a steamer, the first we had seen for three weeks. We were about fifty miles off the Brazilian coast and we aimed to keep off until the time came for us to close the land north of the River Plate. We were pretty confident the coast was there because when we were in the latitude of Recife we had seen in the sky the loom of the lights of a large city.

Off Cape Frio, when the weather became appropriately cool, we found that one of our two big paraffin containers had leaked, so that we had only one gallon left to last us to Montevideo, still a fortnight away. We had therefore to reduce our hot meals to one a day and to forgo steamed puddings. Perhaps it was the denial of these sustaining rib-stickers that made us complain of the increasing cold. If we were feeling cold off the Brazilian coast, what would we feel like twenty degrees further south? The sea temperature had already fallen to 70°F.—no water for weaklings—and only the hardiest of the crew could any longer face the daily rite of three buckets over their heads before breakfast, hail, rain, or shine. Between John and me there lay an unspoken challenge as to which of us would bathe farthest south, and already each was watching the other hopefully for signs of weakening. We began to see more ships. A tanker, the *Ancap Tercero*, passed close and gave us three blasts on her horn. Not to be outdone in civility we replied with three on our hand fog-horn, hiccuping, as it were, in response to a thunder-clap.

On the morning of 28 September, after a fine run of 130 miles before a biting north-east wind, the wind fell light when we were some fifty miles off Cabo Polonio, where we expected to make our landfall. That we were not far from land was evident from the presence of seals. Having sighted what we thought was some wreckage or floating branches and altered course to avoid them, we found a party of seals asleep on their backs with their flippers in the air. Presently we were becalmed, handed the sails, and amused ourselves by watching the antics of a seal and two big gulls. While they sat side by side patiently expectant of scraps from the galley, the seal would suddenly shoot up between them. Squawking indignantly they would flutter off and settle down anew, whereupon the seal would play the same trick. So calm and so inviting was the sea that I rashly dived in before taking its temperature. This proved to be only 56°F.

Meantime the glass had been falling steadily and by morning we were bowling along in thickening weather with a strong southeast wind. Rice pudding for breakfast seemed to me an indication of worse to come. At 11 a.m. we sighted land and a little later identified a lighthouse as that on Cabo Polonio. The thrill and satisfaction of making our appointed landfall, of sighting a new continent after two months at sea, now gave way to concern that we might hit it. With the wind and rain both increasing we spent a most anxious afternoon sailing fast along a lee shore, glimpsing it just often enough to raise doubts as to whether or not we were being set towards it. In the evening a brief clearing showed Cabo Santa Maria abeam, and that we were now well inside the estuary was evident from the nasty, yellow appearance of the water.

The River Plate estuary is 138 miles wide at its mouth, narrowing to fifty-seven miles at Montevideo which is sixty miles from the sea. At its head the estuary is twenty-five miles wide. It receives the waters of six rivers, thus comprising the second largest system in the world. The discolouration caused by the silt can be seen seventy or eighty miles out to sea, while this mingling of tropical river water and the colder water from the southern ocean is marked by the presence of large numbers of petrels, albatrosses, seals, and sometimes penguins. The estuary is noted for its sudden and violent weather changes, for its thunderstorms and dust storms, for *sudestadas*, *zondas*, and *pamperos*, each of which has its own particular unpleasantness. The *pampero* is often preceded by the phenomenon known as *Baba del Diablo*, or Devil's Dribble, which fills the air with the gossamer webs of the aeronaut spider. The *zonda* is a norther; the *pampero*, as its name implies, arises over the pampas and is a line squall which strikes with suddenness and ferocity. The *sudestada*, coming off the sea, brings with it rain and thick weather. Since the estuary is shallow these storms quickly raise a short and nasty sea.

We were about to experience a *sudestada*. Early in the morning after a quiet night the wind rose steadily and heavy rain began driving over

the livid water. For us the wind was fair—a wind the sailor is advised
not to waste—so we shortened sail as far as we could and taking care to
allow two points for leeway we laid a course for the light vessel marking the northern end of the English Bank. This great sandbank lies
plumb in the middle of the estuary and in time past has taken its toll
of many a ship.* This liberal allowance for leeway could be regarded as
a sort of insurance policy, for if the allowance proved to be too much
and so caused us to miss the lightship we might perhaps sight instead
a buoy lying some eight miles to the south. But since the *sudestada* is
accompanied by heavy rain and bad visibility the chances of our sighting a small object like a buoy, which in a rough sea is for half the time
obscured, were not good.

In the early afternoon when we had run our distance and had
sighted nothing, a change of course became imperative if we were to
clear the bank. I had just decided to carry on for another five minutes
when to our joy lynx-eyed Charles sighted the buoy about half a mile
away on our port bow. With renewed confidence we altered course for
the lightship, and at the same time the wind began to moderate and
the rain squalls to become less frequent. For the very good reason that
it was not there the lightship was never found, for as we learnt later it
had been taken off station for repair. However, we soon made out the
Isla de Flores some ten miles to the north, and as we passed the island
a great box-like thing appeared above the distant horizon. At first we
took it for a large ship distorted by mirage—mirage effects are common
in the estuary—but when other rectangular shapes began to show on
either side of it we realised that we were looking at the skyline of Montevideo still some twelve miles away.

As wind and sea subsided we shook out our reefs. Night fell and
we enjoyed a lovely moonlight sail with the lights of the coast road
and the eastern suburbs twinkling close on our starboard hand. At
length we cut into the dredged and buoyed channel where we began to

---

*   Mr J. A. Drever, who has made enquiries for me in Montevideo, cannot
      discover the origin of the name. The oldest document on the subject
      (he writes) is a chart dated 1685, compiled by a pilot of the Royal Span-
      ish Navy called Andred Emaili. On this chart the English Bank already
      figures.

experience one of the problems of entering a strange harbour at night, the picking out of the aids to navigation from among the even brighter aids to dissipation, the neon signs and coloured lights of bars, night clubs, and such like. After an exchange of marine pleasantries with a steamer and its attendant tug in the harbour entrance, we motored in and dropped anchor at 1 a.m. on 1 October, sixty-four days out from Las Palmas and all well. Rum and cocoa were served in the cabin.

CHAPTER V

THE MAGELLAN STRAITS

*We found by a miracle, a strait which we called the Strait of the
Eleven Thousand Virgins. I think there is not a more beautiful country, or a better strait than this one.*

PIGAFETTA

HAVING ENTERED A STRANGE PORT by night one goes on deck
the next morning hopeful as a playgoer watching the curtain
rise on another scene. This state of happy expectancy may perhaps be regarded as some slight recompense for the anxieties of
the night before. But if it is a busy commercial port one's hopes
should not be pitched too high, for in such places few concessions
are made to aesthetic taste. The decor is strictly functional. But
after nine weeks at sea, even a crane is a refreshing sight, while the
majestic view of a grain elevator may move a susceptible seaman
to tears.

The first and obvious thing we noted was our ill-chosen anchorage. Evidently it had been determined upon more by the wish to
have done than by any seamanlike regard for safety. We found ourselves close to some seaplane mooring buoys. The inevitable visit
from some indignant port official was forestalled by Mr J. A. Drever
of Messrs Maclean and Stapledon (the agents who were handling our
twenty-four cases of provisions which had been lying in the customs
since the previous year). He brought with him the port doctor to give
us pratique and showed us a better anchorage. He also told us that
he was arranging that we should lie at Puerto Buceo, the headquarters of the Uruguayan Yacht Club. We were congratulated upon our
ocean crossing. This had proved easier than we had expected, but
any complacency we might have felt was tempered by the thoughts
of the next leg of the journey where the Roaring Forties and the Furious Fifties promised a stiffer test. On the whole the weather had been

kind to us, and a gale of wind in the tropics is not so searching a trial as a gale under the lowering skies and in the colder waters of higher latitudes.

Next day we motored round to Puerto Buceo, a small, snug harbour lying a few miles to the east and occupied solely by yachts and a few fishing boats. The Argentine coast, seventy miles away, appeared as a mirage with its trees floating in the air. Having first taken the ground as we tried to moor to the jetty and later having parted two warps when tied to a trawler, *Mischief* was finally anchored off the Yacht Club where she lay for the next fortnight. Apart from numerous small jobs, the topmast had to be sent down, the clew of the Genoa had to be repaired, and the seams of the mainsail hand-stitched. Since leaving Las Palmas we had constantly to lower the sail for resewing seams which just as constantly opened at some fresh point. It seemed so worth while having the whole sail hand sewn that we struck a bargain with an old coloured sailor. Sitting on a back verandah of the Club, he stitched away happily for ten days until the job was done, and a very good job he made of it. Subsequently we had little trouble with seams opening and still wore the same sail when recrossing the Atlantic the following June. Sewing done by hand is stronger than that done by machine. The stitches are tighter, they sit closer and are therefore less likely to chafe, and if one stitch goes the others are not so liable to pull out as when machine sewn. The high initial cost is the only disadvantage.

In the South Atlantic we should not want to hoist either the topsail or the big Genoa and we should be better off without the weight of the useless topmast aloft. Striking it did not prove so troublesome as we expected. Quite unnecessarily, I thought we ought to lessen the weight by sending down the four wire topmast-stays before starting the spar itself, and consequently I spent a long time at the masthead in a bos'n's chair wrestling with stiff shackles. Had any of us closely examined the topsail halyard from which my chair was suspended before hoisting, I should not have been aloft nearly so long, for one of its strands was found to be chafed through. Having got the topmast down we lashed it on deck. It took up so much room, from abaft the cockpit nearly to the foot of the mast, that we seriously considered leaving it at the Yacht Club until our return. Our plan had always been to return the same way, but, as the great Moltke said, no plan survives contact with the enemy, so we took it with us.

Fourteen days slipped by quickly, each of the crew labouring in his own vocation. Mike became so immersed in the pursuit of local colour and social engagements that we saw little of him. Procter devoted himself to searching for places where one got the most food for the least money, a search for which his fluent Spanish well qualified him and in which his voracity well rewarded him. At times I enjoyed the benefits of this painstaking piece of research. Charles, whose clothes needed constant attention if they were to hold together, fancied himself as a tailor and had begun to make a windproof jacket against the rigours of the ice-cap. To have more light and to give his needle free play he occupied a bedroom on the fourth floor of the Yacht Club's eight-storey building. John divided his time between the ground floor of the club, among the refreshments, and the ship.

We had been given the freedom of the club, a privilege we much appreciated and one which brought us many friends. Among them was the owner of *Blue Disa* which he had sailed out the previous year from England under the Uruguayan flag. She is a sister-ship of the well known ocean-racer *Samuel Pepys*. And there was a Frenchman who lived aboard his modern ketch, sailing round South America, painting scenes of Indian life, and exhibiting his pictures at the larger cities. Another friend, who on our departure made us a present of sugar and butter, was the night watchman, a Pole who had fought in the British Army as a paratrooper. It was remarkable, by the way, the number of Uruguayans with British connections who had come over to fight in the last war. A striking figure always around the club was the bosun, very large, fat, rubicund, and the possessor of a glass eye which at moments of crisis, such as when lifting a yacht out of the water by crane, he popped in his mouth for safety. Many of the club members seemed to have two jobs, neither of which occupied much of their time and one of which was usually connected with the press. We were invited to the offices of *El Pais* where at four in the afternoon we were regaled with whisky and nuts, and interviewed amid manifold interruptions from telephone calls and other business. The printing machinery would have been more impressive had it been working or had our guide had any inkling of what the machines did or how they worked.

My visits to the city were always on business and I always slept on board. (In the course of our year's wanderings I spent only one night ashore under a roof.) In Montevideo I noted a refreshing absence of uniforms, for Uruguay is a free country in every sense—free trade, free currency, free speech. Everyone abuses the government or lack of government, but the principle of giving the other side a turn is well understood. It is the only Welfare State, I understand, in South America. More remarkable is the fact that it has nine Presidents. To me this provision seemed unnecessary in Uruguay, but in more effervescent countries it would be wise enough, for there is safety in numbers. I was impressed by the vast grandeur of the cemetery; the whole surrounded by a high wall with massive iron gates built with a view to baffling body-snatchers. And mention of the cemetery reminds me of another curious building looking exactly like a mosque, from whose history there is a moral to be drawn if philosophy could but find it out. It began life soberly enough as a crematorium, blazed garishly for a short time as a night club until its flames were extinguished, presumably by the police, when it reverted to the housing of dust and ashes and became a museum. But strangest of all was the sight of workmen lighting fires on the pavement on which they broiled great slabs of inch-thick steaks for their 'elevenses'. Montevideo is celebrated for its bathing beaches which, in spite of the coolness of the water and its queer colour, attract many visitors from Buenos Aires.

A few days before we were due to sail Charles complained of a stiff shoulder. He decided that he was not fit enough to make the voyage and that he would travel overland to rejoin us at Punta Arenas. Although four of us could manage *Mischief* it meant harder work and should we meet heavy weather in the South Atlantic we should be inconveniently short-handed. A young German, Gird Breuer, who had often been on board had expressed a wish to come with us to Punta Arenas. He had come out to America as a deckhand with a view to learning English and Spanish before joining his father in business. At 1 p.m. on the Saturday when we were to sail I got a message through to him to say that we had a vacant berth. By 4 p.m. he had sacked himself, gathered his few belongings together, and joined *Mischief*.

The trouble about sea voyaging is that you have to start from some port. Throughout the voyage sailing time became more and more a nightmare. There was the last minute round-up on shore, the paying of duty calls, the settling of bills and making forgotten purchases. On board presents arrive and must be acknowledged, hilarious visitors must be persuaded to leave, and finally a hilarious crew must be persuaded to come. We got away before dusk, motoring through the narrow entrance and then sailing close-hauled for the 'Practicos-Recalada' light vessel, twelve miles to the south-west. This is the light vessel at the entrance of the dredged channel to Buenos Aires where ships bound for that place take on or drop their pilot. At midnight we passed close by it, altered course for Cabo San Antonio at the mouth of the estuary on the south side, and streamed the log.

The wind being light from the south-east we did not bring the cape abeam until midnight on the Monday, thus our calm, dignified progress out of the estuary was in marked contrast to the angry fury of our entrance. We had time to complain of the cold, for young Gird to be sea-sick, and for some successful fishing. In the shallow water of the estuary we caught no less than sixteen fish of about 1 lb. each of a species known locally as *palometa*. And outside the estuary, while becalmed off Punta Medanos in shoal water, we were able to catch as many as we wanted of a variety called *pescadilla*—a fish bigger than the *palometa* and round like a whiting. They were bottom feeders which took anything from a bare hook to rags, feathers, or a bit of fish. Shallow water is undoubtedly the place for fish; we never had fishing like that again. In the course of the whole voyage we caught only about a dozen dorado and it always seemed to me that in mid-ocean the chances of catching fish at any particular moment were little better than the chance of catching a mermaid.

The 1200-odd miles from Montevideo to Punta Arenas proved to be our slowest passage giving an average of only fifty-six miles a day. For the first six days we scarcely made thirty miles a day and that only by dint of using the motor in flat calms. They were pleasant, cool sunny days with plenty to see. On a day of glassy calm the S.S. *Fitzroy* bound for Port Stanley in the Falkland Islands ranged close enough alongside for us to speak by megaphone and offered to report our progress to the British Consul, Punta Arenas. Bird and fish life became more plentiful, if seals, porpoises, and whales may be called fish. The last named, great ugly brutes of from twenty to thirty feet

The 'frigorifico' in Gregory Bay at the eastern end of the Magellan Straits; the flat, barren table land behind is typical of the coast of the mainland at the eastern end of the straits

Punta Arenas: The appropriately desolate-looking 'Bar Antartica' with the jetty and one of the oil companies' landing craft behind; the usual wind is blowing

in length, with high dorsal fins, were identified as killer whales. For the first time we saw penguins and the black and white speckled cape pigeon which followed us right down to the Straits in small flocks of anything up to twenty. The so-called cape pigeon, one of the forty different kinds of petrel, was the only ocean bird we met with which fed readily on scraps. Albatross would follow the ship in their effort-less flight or sometimes sit close by on the water watching us pass and showing not the least interest when the gash bucket was emptied or biscuits thrown over-side. Perhaps they would have taken a lump of pork or fish had we had it to offer, for the catching of albatross with line and hook was once a common sport on sailing ships in spite of the superstition of old sailors. Apparently in those days the price of albatross skins in a place like Melbourne was high enough to over-come any superstitious fears they may have had.

The albatross did not come up to our expectations. Before reluc-tantly concluding that these birds were indeed albatross we must have seen hundreds which, though large, failed to measure up to our ideas. A bird with a wing span of 10 to 15 ft. should, we thought, appear unmistakably huge, and we were constantly calling one another up from below to pass judgment upon some newcomer—whether, or not he qualified as a genuine wandering albatross. Our imaginations had so bodied forth the form of things unknown that we refused to believe what we saw and still looked for bigger and better birds farther south. At the other end of the scale were the tiny storm petrels. These are the size of a swallow and are the most widespread, companionable, and reassuring of ocean birds. To see such a small bird hundreds of miles from land in stormy weather pursuing his busy, erratic flight, liter-ally dancing on the waves, is most comforting. These are the Mother Carey's chickens of the sailor, Mother Carey being, I believe, a corrup-tion of Mater Cara, an appellation of the Blessed Virgin. Both in the North and South Atlantic and in the Pacific oceans there were few days when Mother Carey's chickens were not seen, so that had one believed that their presence foreboded stormy weather one would have led a most unquiet life.

This tranquil bird-watching life was rudely interrupted when out of a profound calm a sharp gale sprang at us from the south-east. Her-alded by a swiftly advancing bank of mist the first puffs increased in a matter of minutes to gale force, compelling us to reef right down and finally to change to trysail, double reefed staysail and storm jib, a rig under which we passed a cold and stormy night. By the following after-noon the wind had dropped enough for us to reset the working sails but with two rolls in the mainsail. The sea was still running very high and young Gird was sick. For that matter so was I, perhaps because of having had soup for lunch or because of the mental exertion of work-ing out sights which is apt to make a weak head spin. After this shak-ing up we watched the slow downward curve of the barograph with apprehension. However, it was still above normal for those waters and in the event we enjoyed a succession of clear, fine days with fair winds. It was becoming markedly and steadily colder, the sea and air tempera-tures having dropped to 48°F. and 49°F. respectively.

After passing the great gulfs of San Matias and San George we closed the land in the vicinity of Cabo Blanco (there must be a dozen capes bearing this unimaginative name) and on the morning of 31 October we raised the low, barren coast to the south of the cape. An Argentine frigate came out of Puerto Deseado, Port Desire, and soon we were able to identify Penguin Island some ten miles to the south. It was at Puerto Deseado that 'penguins' were first given their name by a Welshman sailing with Sir Thomas Cavendish. He called them 'pen gwyn' which is, of course, the Welsh for white head. Penguin Isle is the place where the great seaman and navigator John Davis, having been parted from Cavendish on their second voyage to the Straits, revict-ualled his ship *Desire* for the voyage back to England. They took on board 14,000 dried penguins. For an estimated voyage of six months this gave a daily ration of five penguins for four men, but long before they reached England (which they did in six months) this vast stock of imperfectly dried meat had gone rotten. The stores, the ship, the men themselves became infested with maggots—'there was nothing,' wrote John Jane who was one of the crew, 'they did not devour, only iron excepted.' When the noisome, worm-ridden *Desire* struggled into Bearhaven in June 1593 only sixteen of her crew remained alive and of these only five were able to stand.

Between Puerto Deseado and Cape Virgins there lies a long stretch of desolate, wind-swept coast, upon which there are only two small ports used mainly for the seasonal shipments of frozen mutton and wool. Besides being remarkable for strong tides with a great range—at Port San Julian the range is as much as 45ft.—these two places are of historic interest. San Julian, 100 miles south of Deseado, is the place where after a violent mutiny Magellan executed two of its leaders and marooned two others, one a priest. Here Drake, sixty years later, had John Doughty beheaded, and before continuing the voyage made a harangue to his crew in which he offered the faint-hearted a ship to return home in and uttered the oft quoted words: 'For I must have the gentlemen to haul and draw with the mariners, and the mariners with the gentlemen; and let us show ourselves to be all of a company, and let us not give occasion to the enemy to rejoice at our decay and over-throw. I would know him that would refuse to set his hand to a rope; but I trust there is not any such here.'

Sixty miles further down the coast from San Julian is Santa Cruz lying at the mouth of the Santa Cruz river which rises in Lake Argen-tino. When the *Beagle* on her famous voyage round the world anchored there in 1834 Captain Fitzroy with a party of twenty-five, including the young Darwin, set out in three whale boats to explore the river. For eighteen days these indomitable seamen hauled their heavy boats against a five-knot current; and then having reached a point about 140 miles from the sea they turned back and regained the ship in only three days, so powerful was the current. Had they persevered for another day, or at most two, they would have been the first Europeans to discover Lake Argentino. But for several days they had been on half rations and as Darwin wrote in his account: 'A light stomach and easy digestion are good to talk about but very unpleasant in practice.' J. H. Gardiner was the first to reach Lake Argentino thirty-three years later, in 1867. Dar-win's own ability as a traveller, his toughness and endurance in accom-plishing long journeys on foot or on horseback, and his venturesome spirit, are sometimes overlooked.

Now that we were well down in the forties the South Atlantic began to roar to some purpose. No sooner had we left Penguin Isle astern than the coast vanished in a murky haze, while to the south, clouds (which, by the way, I noted in my diary as 'not very threatening') began to gather. The gale struck with stunning force. By evening we were run-ning before it to the Magellan Straits north-east under bare poles. But its first fury did not last, for in the course of the night, a glorious night of full moon and cloudless sky, we were able to set the trysail and get the ship once more heading south. By daylight the wind had veered to the north and we got up all plain sail. But again the wind freshened, and again the mainsail had to give way to trysail and storm jib, and later, as she was running too fast, to the jib alone. But at least we were running in the right direction, and *Mischief* had shewn herself to be such an able sea-boat that we had no anxiety on her account. After two days of better weather, when we were twenty miles off the entrance to the Straits, the glass fell to 29" and the wind rose. We made our landfall under the conditions which we had now come to regard as specially reserved for such occasions. At 2 a.m. on the morning of 5 November, with a strong westerly gale blowing, we sighted the Cape Virgins light, a little to the north of the entrance to the Straits. Daylight revealed a long, flat line of white cliffs, except for the lighthouse on the eastern extremity bare as the sea itself. The wind was blowing straight out of the Straits and a high, confused sea was running. We could make no westing so we hove to on the starboard tack and drifted slowly southward. In the evening, with no land in sight, we went about to recover our ground and at midnight we once more raised the light. And so it went on. We stood off until the evening of the 6th, when the wind moderating, we shook out all reefs and stood in to the south-west.

Off the entrance to the Straits the tidal streams are strong and confusing; for the flood stream makes north up the coast from round the Horn and also sets east through the Straits, and in the same way the ebb running south divides, part of it setting west through the Straits. So when the wind fell light we started the engine, fully determined that no false pride should stop us entering the Straits and attaching ourselves firmly to the bottom to save our being blown out or set out by the tide. Bernicot, who in 1936 in the cutter *Anahita* had repeated Slocum's single-handed circumnavigation by way of the Magellan Straits, had had a rough handling just inside the entrance and was twice swept out to sea in spite of all that sail and engine could do. Slocum, too, had no sooner rounded Cape Virgins than a south-westerly gale struck him and for thirty hours his sloop *Spray* managed to hold her ground with no more than a three-reefed mainsail and forestaysail. She had no engine and she was not driven out to sea; but then *Spray* was *Spray* and there have been few seamen like Slocum.

Inside the Straits the tidal streams are stronger and reach their maximum strength in the First and Second Narrows. In the First Narrows spring tides run at from five to eight knots and are not much less in the Second Narrows. Between the eastern entrance and Punta Arenas a sailing vessel or a low-powered steamer must therefore work the tides, anchoring when the stream is against her. By 10 o'clock that night, when the Dungeness light bore north, we knew we were fairly inside the Straits, and with a nice breeze coming in from north-west and with the flood under us we sailed happily westwards gaining assurance with every mile made good. Early in the morning, when the ebb began to run, we dropped anchor at the tail of the Orange Bank.

Coming on deck that morning with the vague, mysterious coast of Tierra del Fuego on one side and the bold headland of Cape Possession on the other, we felt our adventure had really begun. Until the tide turned we fished unsuccessfully and watched with interest some Commerson's dolphins. These were the first we had seen; they are smaller than most dolphins with black and white colouring sharply delimited, the white part including the flippers and the lower half of the head. When the flood began to make we weighed and stood towards Punta Delgada at the entrance to the First Narrows. As we neared it the wind dropped so we started the engine and with the tide running full bore we swept through the Narrows with a speed of something like eight knots over the ground. The channel has a least width of two miles, the fairway is deep, and the shores steep-to but not high. An hour later we shot out of the western end and at the same time the engine failed. There was no wind but the tide still ran strongly enough to carry us to a safe anchorage in Santiago Bay.

Instead of pressing on that night with the next tide we took a long night in. At noon next day we weighed again hoping to pass the Second Narrows while it was still light, for at this time of year it is light until after 10 o'clock. No sooner had we started, however, than the wind came in so strongly from dead ahead that we had to push the engine hard to get as far as Gregory Bay, the next anchorage some ten miles to the west. In Gregory Bay there is a *frigorifico*, a mere collection of buildings with a tall, iron chimney and a wood jetty from which the frozen mutton is shipped. We anchored close off the end of the jetty where only a few children gathered to look at the strange ship, for at this time of year the place was not being used. As if a *frigorifico* was not a strong enough hint that times had changed we could see, as we looked across the Straits that night, the great flames of natural gas from the oil wells on Tierra del Fuego. Thus the voyager in these historic waters, aglow with such romantic names as Famine Reach, Royal Road, Pelican Passage, or Elizabeth Island (so named by Drake), whose imagination has been stirred and who yet cherishes the hopeful illusion that the low coast on either hand is still wild and strange, must here abandon such imaginings, now utterly extinguished by the horrid reality of a *frigorifico* on the one hand and of oil derricks on the other.

Expecting to reach Punta Arenas that day we got under way soon after midnight. Since the Second Narrows are much wider than the First the stream is weaker. In our eagerness to be off we rounded Gregory Point and were at the entrance of the channel before the east-going stream had stopped running. Until the tide turned progress was slow, but by five in the morning, when it was full day, we had cleared the western end. As we altered course for Punta Arenas, for the Straits here bend sharply southwards, we met a rare sailing breeze from the north-west. The day was wonderfully clear. To starboard lay Drake's well-wooded Elizabeth Island, with Queen Channel to the east of it and Royal Road and Pelican Passage to the west. Ahead Broad Reach opened out, its light blue waters ruffled by the freshening wind. Beyond it to the south lay high ground, the slopes green with forest and crowned with patches of winter snow. Far away in the distance, from west round to south, rose a jagged skyline of high mountains, the highest of them glistening with the convincing whiteness of perpetual ice and snow. So unexpected a vision was heartening. There at any rate was country still wild and strange.

As the wind gradually freshened and Broad Reach became covered with white-capped waves, *Mischief* sped along with a bone in her teeth as if eager to finish in style what had been a rather slow passage. The brown huddle at the foot of a bleak, reddish coloured hillside which we had long decided was Punta Arenas began to take shape. In the roads a big four-masted hulk lay forlorn and uncared for, and soon we could make out the jetty and we had to decide where to go. We were still sailing fast, a little too fast for accurate navigation, and presently a jar and a shudder warned us that *Mischief* had indeed reached

Patagonia. But in a matter of minutes she had bumped over the shoal and we lost no time in handing the sail and dropping anchor a cable's length from the jetty. A pilot launch was soon alongside and towed us to the jetty where we tied up. We had at any rate astonished the natives. The slight *contretemps* had gone unnoticed by the ancient mariners and longshoremen who had gathered to see us come in, and who, as we heard later, had much admired our dashing approach, swift rounding-to and stowing of sails. To have made such an impression was gratifying, for it is not every day that an English yacht, or indeed any yacht, comes to Punta Arenas. It was perhaps a pity that our departure was destined to be the reverse of dashing.

CHAPTER VI

PUNTA ARENAS

Bright and fierce and fickle is the South.

TENNYSON

IN THESE REGIONS Punta Arenas is the last outpost of civilization. As Sir Fopling Flutter remarked of Hyde Park, 'beyond that all is desert'. Along the coast for 500 or 600 miles west and north there are no settlements, and although the *South America Pilot* states that 'the greater part is inhabited by savages of the lowest civilization', this is, unhappily, no longer true. In the three months we spent in the channels we did not have the good fortune to sight one of their canoes or to hear their poignant cry of 'yammerschooner' (the Canoe Indian's word for 'bakhshish'), the cry which sixty years before had so disgusted Captain Slocum. Had we come across any of these despised savages they could have done nothing for us except possibly to pose for their photographs. They could neither have carried loads for us nor provided any food, so that the problems of mountain travel in this region are less easily solved than in the Himalaya where even in the remotest valley it is usually possible to find food and transport.

Punta Arenas, or Magallanes as it is known, had therefore to be the base where we must make our final arrangements. Once we had left it behind, although we should always be in sight of land, we might as well be in mid-ocean; nor had we any means of communication—an advantage, perhaps, in enterprises of this kind. A Commander F. J. Porta of the Chilean Naval Mission at that time in England, had recommended me to the care of the naval authorities at Punta Arenas and they now gave us all the help they could. As a first instalment we made use of the hot shower baths of a naval tug lying at the jetty. Our brass tiller was badly bent so we handed it to a Lieutenant Hudson of this same tug that it might be sent to the arsenal to be straightened and to have a sleeve brazed on. As there is a rule that all foreign vessels navigating

the channels must take a Chilean pilot, the naval authorities had contemplated sending Lieutenant Hudson with us. We should have been
delighted to have him, both for his own sake and for his knowledge
of the channels. But had he come the authorities would have had to
arrange for him to be taken off by another ship after we had reached
Peel Inlet, and in addition *Mischief* turned out to be not quite the type
of vessel they were expecting. After consulting naval headquarters in
Valparaiso they waived the rule and we were allowed to sail without
a pilot. The navy also helped us with petrol. For navigating the channels we had always intended making full use of our engine. In places
they are narrow, the prevailing wind is from the north, and we should
have to enter and anchor in many small, rock-strewn coves. Neither
had we much time in hand; so that on all counts it seemed desirable
to take all the petrol we could. I decided to take two 40-gal. drums on
deck—a fairly safe cargo because except for one short reach off Tamar
Island the channels are so sheltered that there are no big seas to fear.
These drums and our tanks gave us a range of about 500 miles. As this
was not enough for the journey to Peel Inlet and back again, the navy
promised that if a ship were going that way it would leave a drum of
petrol for us at Puerto Bueno. As will appear, they were better than
their word.

The Honorary British Consul (T. P. Jones, Esq., M.B.E.) and members of the British community were most helpful and kind. Unluckily
not all of us could accept the hospitality offered, especially the invi-
tations to estancias on the mainland or on Tierra del Fuego, because
there had always to be enough crew on board to tend the warps and
if necessary to move the ship from the jetty. As an old sea captain
remarked, Punta Arenas has a strong climate. On most days in summer
it blows hard, sometimes very hard; and in winter, although there is
less wind, it is very cold. The prevailing wind is off the land, but the
roadstead feels its full force and there is not much shelter in the lee of
the jetty. Big sailing ships naturally avoided the Straits, going always
by Cape Horn, but among the port regulations still quoted in the *South
America Pilot* is one that shows what might be expected: 'Whenever the
weather is bad, vessels anchored in the port must let go their second
anchor, hoist their boats, haul in their guess-warp booms, send down
top-gallant masts, and point their yards to the wind.'

On the afternoon after our arrival the wind, normally a pretty vigorous blast, showed signs of becoming something more. Our tiller, it will be remembered, was ashore for repair so that there was no casting off and anchoring in the roads. By dark it was blowing a whole gale and several warps had already parted. Constructed of open timber work the jetty gave little shelter. We were on the lee side but in effect there was no lee for the wind whistled straight through underneath the decking. We had an ample reserve of warps but thinking to fix things once and for all we shackled a length of wire rope to the jetty, led it in over the bow and round the bitts, out over the stern, and shackled that end as well to the jetty. By the time this had been done *Mischief*, lying broadside to the jetty, had been blown far enough from it to prevent anyone getting ashore. Thus, for better or for worse, we were wedded to the jetty by this infernal piece of wire—a wire most unlikely to part for it had been used in raising the Comet aircraft which had crashed off Sicily. We soon found it was to be for worse. The wire began to saw its way into the stemhead and anything it touched. The bitts began to move and life-line stanchions to bend. There was no casting it off—the strain on it saw to that. Shackled as we were to an inaccessible jetty there was no way of freeing ourselves short of cutting the wire. But by midnight something had to be done. Procter offered to haul himself ashore along one of our remaining warps but I thought this a too risky manoeuvre and refused.

Only a few yards ahead of us lay the brightly lit naval tug, snuggly secure in a cocoon of warps. Its two men on watch at first were not aware of the dramatic entertainment going on close under their stern, but presently it occurred to them that all was was not well with us. Through the howling of the gale, by means of signs and shrieks, we made them understand what was wanted. Since they had no marline spike for undoing the shackles we passed one over on a line, and then sent them the end of our anchor chain to make fast to the jetty. When the strain was on the chain they were able to unshackle the wire, and we then paid out the chain and rode comfortably, well clear of the jetty, for what little remained of the night. Dawn disclosed a haggard trio.

After this all-night performance we moored ourselves on the lee side of a big L.C.T., an ex-wartime tank landing craft, one of several which were used by the oil company on Tierra del Fuego for landing stores. There we lay quietly enough until the wind decided to blow from another quarter—on to the land from the south-east instead of from the north-west. This sent in such a swell that one after another our fenders began to go, either by being ground to bits against the plates of the L.C.T. or by getting caught under her rubbing strake and breaking their lines. One of these I was particularly sorry to lose because recently I had devoted several days and much loving care to covering its canvas with coir 'needle-stitching'. But now we had our tiller back and after some delay in starting the engine, for the battery was down, we cast off and motored out to anchor west of the jetty. Had it not been for the necessity of going ashore it would have been well to stay there, but on most days it would have been difficult to row ashore, with only an even chance of rowing back. A good friend then gave us three rubber tyres for fenders and we were allotted a better berth at the shore end of the jetty where a steamer lying on the other side made an excellent wind-break.

This desirable berth became vacant through the departure of the spider crab fishing boats, their season having just begun. The spider crab, known locally as *centolla*, is a speciality of these waters. It is large, deep red in colour, and has spidery legs covered with spiny protuberances. We thought its meat far more delicious than that of any other crab and enjoyed them both fresh and tinned. There are canning factories at Punta Arenas and across the Straits at Porvenir and considerable quantities are exported. This crab, I believe, is akin to that species of king crab fished for in the North Pacific and off the Alaskan coast. In the Magellan Straits they catch it in nets in deep water—as deep as thirty fathoms, we were told.

In spite of telegrams to Santiago and Buenos Aires I had as yet heard nothing of Charles' whereabouts, nor had any Chilean climbers volunteered. It was beginning to look as if the effective shore party would consist only of myself, but as a precautionary measure I bought a pair of climbing boots for Michael. In the long night watches at sea, as I pondered upon this and that, whether physical evil is a cause of moral good or why Procter could not relieve the wheel in time, a constantly recurring question was, when the shore party finally did land after so many months at sea, whether or no its members would have the use of their legs and if not how many days would it take them to recover that use. Now that I had the opportunity I thought it would be wise to try out my own legs and to start fettling up a little.

Inland from the town the ground rises gradually to a flat ridge about a thousand feet high. The forest of oak and Antarctic beech which at one time covered the slopes has since been felled and now there are a few poor farms with wire-fenced fields where cows and a few horses graze. Beyond the farms and below the ridge is a club hut and ski run which is much used in winter. Having visited the ski hut by car on our first day in port I made that my early morning walk. These cross-country walks, climbing over wire fences and seeing nothing but a few haggard hares, were more of a duty than a pleasure, but it was an agreeable surprise to find that I could do the five miles up to the hut and return to the ship without falling or fainting by the way. Leaving the jetty, passing by a saloon of severe aspect appropriately named the 'Bar Antartica', and under the statue of General O'Higgins (like most South American towns Punta Arenas is liberally sprinkled with statues), one soon reached the deplorable suburbs, wooden shanties, and shacks made of flattened petrol tins, reminiscent of the native quarter of Nairobi forty years ago. As with most developing towns the money is dropped in the centre with a big splash and only faint ripples ever reach the outskirts. The centre of Punta Arenas is well laid out in squares, is clean, and has an air of spacious freshness, largely attributable, one supposes, to the incessant wind.

My only other excursion outside the town was to Rio Seco, the oldest *frigorifico* in Magallanes. As the season had not yet begun there were no sheep to be slaughtered and one could view the silent, immaculate works without the unnerving clamour of a season in full swing. Sheep are, of course, the mainstay of Patagonia and of Tierra del Fuego. That part of Patagonia which belongs to Chile is known as the province of Magallanes, but only the southern part near the Straits is inhabited. The province also includes the western end of Tierra del Fuego, the eastern end of the island belonging to the Argentine. Punta Arenas is the capital and the centre from which the great quantities of wool, frozen meat, and skins are shipped.

While waiting one afternoon for the museum to open, Michael and I spent the time in the next best thing, the cemetery. This presented some novel features. In spite of the bracing climate the graves were well supplied with flowers. Indeed, provided they are screened from the shrivelling wind, European flowers and vegetables thrive out of doors. But in some cases the owner of the grave, as distinct from its occupant, had taken the precaution of building a conservatory or hothouse over it. Some of the vaults were most impressive. In addition to the wealthy families (and some of the families of the early settlers are very wealthy indeed), the police, the army, the navy, and several mutual or co-operative burial societies, had its own vault wherein the neatly labelled drawers or niches round the walls reminded one of a filing cabinet.

The inhabitants, of whom there are now some 35,000, have a weather-beaten air, as well they might. Apart from the business community they are essentially the descendants of gauchos, sailors, convicts, ship-wrecked mariners, gold seekers, sea otter and seal hunters, Alacaluf Indians, Onas, Yaghans, and such like tough *hombres*. The very few indigenes or semi-indigenes seen in the streets were thick-set and short, of high colour, and with thick black hair. Evidently they were no kin to those original inhabitants of gigantic stature whom Magellan met and to whom he gave the name Patagones or 'big feet'.

In its palmiest days Punta Arenas was a more cosmopolitan town or city, for nowadays the majority of its population are of Chilean extraction. It was the British who first introduced sheep and who started the sheep farms both on the mainland and on Tierra del Fuego. When the shipping business of the port was at its height in the years before the opening of the Panama Canal, the British community practically ran the place. More English than Spanish was spoken; wages were paid in sterling and many of the stores marked their prices in sterling. An amusing reminder of this bygone influence are the signs still to be seen over some of the smaller workshops, the 'Gasfiteria' or 'Tinplateria'. The chief engineer of a ship is still known as a 'chiffinger'. One of the old inhabitants who had experienced these halcyon days told me that then there was neither Army, Navy, nor Custom House; that the poorest workman smoked Abdullas, and that whisky and French Champagne cost five shillings a bottle. Can one imagine conditions more conducive to the peace, prosperity, and tranquillity of mankind?

A less amusing relic of those days is the British Club which, like many clubs nearer home, now faces a dwindling membership. On the

other hand the Golf Club, the most southerly in the world, where a
player might well think himself on the ringing plains of windy Troy, is
by no means moribund. There all nations are welcome; Germans, Ital-
ians, Frenchmen, Yugo Slavs, and Turks, not to mention Chileans, may
drive balls into the sea as freely as any Englishman, Scot, or Welshman. Now, of all the foreigners, the Yugo Slavs are the most numerous. The early comers, then known as Austriacos, were of peasant stock
from the Dalmatian coast. Their immigration had been accelerated by
the annexation of Bosnia and Hercegovina in 1908. Many of them took
to washing gold on the beaches (where a good day's pay can still be
made), while others took up land. Some of these early settlers became
very rich and today their descendants are prosperous doctors, lawyers,
and business men.

In the British Club there is an interesting relic in the form of
Admiral Cradock's visiting card which he left when on his way to the
disastrous battle of Coronel. And there is also a living relic of those stir-
ring times, an old German sea captain Albert Pagels. In the Falkland
Islands battle of 8 October 1914, the sequel to Coronel, all the German
ships in South American waters were sunk except the cruiser *Dresden*
which escaped to Punta Arenas. After twenty-four hours (in which, I
believe, she managed to coal) she had to clear out. She took refuge in
Cockburn channel where for many months she lay hid, playing a successful game of hide-and-seek in these intricate channels, being vict-
ualled and in other ways aided by our friend Pagels who owned a small
cutter. Eventually, in March 1915, she was found at Juan Fernandez
where she blew herself up. Before this interesting episode Pagels had
accompanied the Skottsberg expedition as guide and handyman and
finished by travelling on horseback right down the eastern side of the
Cordillera from Aysen to Punta Arenas. No doubt in the intervening
years he had other notable adventures, but he next appears as a public
hero (thanks to the *Dresden* exploit) in Hitler's Germany just before
the war. Indestructibly tough, he took part in this war, too, and having
been captured by, and escaped from, the Russians (whom he does not
like) he returned to Punta Arenas where he was one of the first to welcome *Mischief*.

In Punta Arenas we found plenty of good shops but all suffering
from the effects of rigorous import restrictions. With few exceptions

everything sold had to be made or grown in Chile. The most welcome presents one could make were things like tea, mustard, golden syrup, fruit salts; and English tobacco or cigarettes were unobtainable. I was always trying to cadge tobacco (British ships being the chief sufferers) while John was reduced to cigarettes of local tobacco rolled in *The Times* airmail edition. Compared with the same edition of the *Daily Telegraph* it was in this respect alone well worth the extra money. These import restrictions, applicable to the whole of Chile, appeared not to be uniformly enforced. Punta Arenas, small, uninfluential, and furthest from Santiago, suffered them in full measure. The current rumour that it was about to be declared a free port was bred, perhaps, by wishful thinking. Our twenty-three cases of provisions from Montevideo 'in transit' had been clutched by the customs and much time, trouble and money had to be spent before we were allowed to take half on board and consign the remainder to Valparaiso. By now we had revised our plan of returning by the same route, a thing always to be avoided if possible. This change became possible mainly because we were ahead of schedule. The governing factor was that we must be clear of the West Indies before the beginning of the hurricane season in July, and provided no undue delays occurred we should be able to go up the west coast, through the canal, and be out of the Caribbean before then.

By now we had been in port nearly a week. We had filled up with water and taken on board the two drums of petrol; but still there was no news from Charles. At last on the 16th I had a letter to say he proposed coming from Valdivia by a steamer and was due to arrive on 26 November. As we had planned to sail on the 20th I cabled him to fly from Puerto Montt just south of Valdivia, and in order to clinch the matter and forestall argument (for I recollected that Charles mistrusted air travel) booked and paid for his seat. Over the weekend the office staff of the airline (who behaved very well) had a trying time. I pestered them daily for news of our wandering boy and for passenger lists of incoming planes. Puerto Montt reported that a bearded figure in a yachting cap had put in a brief appearance, the rest was silence. Finally, to our disgust, we learnt from the shipping company that he had in fact embarked on the S.S. *Arica* as he originally intended. Accordingly sailing day had to be deferred to the 26th. It seems that on the way to the air-field something told him that he would not reach

Punta Arenas that day—a premonition that proved perfectly correct as he had no intention of embarking and allowed the aircraft to depart without him.

Meantime from Santiago there came news of a volunteer for the shore party. A young Chilean climber, Jorge Quinteros, recommended by the 'Federation Andinismo de Chile', offered to come. He had climbed in the Central Andes and was a student of ballet and a bee-keeper. He spoke little or no English. He was prepared to fly to Punta Arenas for an interview without any commitment on my part, but I felt that if he came as far as that I could hardly send him back. So I decided to take him. After all a ballet dancer should have impeccable balance and Everest had been climbed by a bee-keeper. But in asking him I made it clear that there would be a great deal more load carrying than climbing and that he would be away at least three months. When Jorge arrived on the 24th he did not seem much disconcerted by the rum-looking characters with whom he had thrown in his lot, by what to his eyes must have been the inadequate size of *Mischief*, or by the rather cramped bunk in which he was invited to spread himself and his gear. I think that thus to commit himself inescapably for a period of three months in the company of strangers and foreigners, in the totally unfamiliar circumstances of a small yacht bound on a voyage of some hazard, required more than common spirit. I am glad to say this gamble came off. I don't think Jorge ever regretted having joined us and our only regret was when he left. On the ship, of course, he was able to converse with Procter who put him in the way of things and told him what had to be done. On the ice-cap journey talking was not so easy, but there are occasions when it is an advantage not to be able to exchange ideas—'the camel driver has his thoughts, and the camel he has his'.

On the morning of the 26th the S.S. *Arica* came alongside the jetty bringing with her our missing tourist. Sailing time was fixed for 2 o'clock. At 2.30 p.m. the crew began to assemble and by 3 p.m. we were complete, a search party having retrieved John from the Hotel de France where he was playing the piano. By then a large crowd of friends, admirers, and no doubt some critics, had assembled to see us start. After some hasty last-minute photography we hoisted the jib so that her head would sheer away from the jetty, and cast off the remaining warps. For some as yet unexplained reason the jib promptly fell into the sea and the next minute saw us stuck hard and fast by the stern less than a ship's length from the waving crowd. The wise man sits on the hole in his carpet, but there was no covering our shame; the critics would need neither telescopes nor binoculars to discern our embarrassment. Having recovered the jib and unavailingly tried the engine which we had hitherto been too proud to use, we sent a warp ashore to the accompaniment of much friendly advice from the experts with the idea of pulling her off the mud. *Mischief*, who had so eagerly taken the ground on her arrival, seemed to have a liking for the place and would not budge. In the roads two Chilean cruisers lay at anchor and at this moment of crisis one of their picket boats was approaching the jetty at the good round pace common to picket boats, a sailor with a boathook standing rigidly to attention in the bow. Either by seamanlike intuition or at the instance of the loud instructions from the crowd, her helmsman grasped the idea that we wanted pulling off. Perhaps he thought we wanted shoving off, for putting his helm hard over, with little diminution of speed, he rammed us fair and square, projecting the still rigid, well-disciplined bowman halfway up our shrouds. It was a Saturday afternoon and one could almost hear the happy sigh of the crowd as they realised how wise they had been to spend it on the jetty. However, the aquatic sports were nearly over. With admirable fortitude *Mischief* uncomplainingly sustained this assault and rather surprisingly remained unmoved. But by now we had a line to the still quivering picket boat which, forging ahead, plucked us quickly into deeper water. With all speed we hoisted sail. Rounding the jetty and dipping our ensign to the cruisers, we headed south.

CHAPTER VII

THE MAGELLAN STRAITS
Western End

This streight is extreme cold; the trees seeme to stoope with the burden of the weather and yet are greene continually. Towards the South sea monstrous high hills and craggy rocks do exalt themselves, whose lops be all hoary with snow.

HAKLUYT'S 'VOYAGES'

STILL SOUTHWARDS! We had yet fifty miles to go before we could round Cape Froward, the southernmost point of the American continent in lat. 53°56"S. We were sailing down Broad Reach which continues south of Punta Arenas and is some twenty miles wide. Gradually it narrows and leads into Famine Reach where the Straits are only five miles wide. As if to atone for the shambles of her departure *Mischief*, with two rolls in the mainsail, went down Broad Reach at a great clip. The flat, barren coasts of the eastern end gave way to bold, densely wooded shores, while to the south rose the wild, snow-covered peaks of Dawson Island. We looked in vain for the twin summits of Mount Sarmiento (7,215 ft.), the highest peak of Tierra del Fuego and a worthy memorial to one of the bravest, most unfortunate, and most indefatigable of seamen. I like to think I once saw this peak from Punta Arenas. At that time it had not been climbed and few attempts have been made since 1898, when Lord Conway with two Swiss guides, who first set foot on it, attained a height of 4000 feet. Had we returned by Punta Arenas I would have had a closer look at it, but in the following February, when we were in the Pacific, the peak was climbed by an Italian party organised by the veteran Alberto de Agostini S.D.B., a man who has done more exploration in Tierra del Fuego and the Patagonian Andes than anyone. In the evening, as the wind had freshened to force 7, we took another roll in the mainsail, reefed the staysail, and

set the storm jib. It was a short-lived flurry; by midnight we were drifting past the Santa Ana lighthouse with barely steerage way. Santa Ana
is one of the headlands enclosing a small bay and anchorage known
as Port Famine, the last good anchorage for vessels bound west before
rounding Cape Froward. It is not a port and no one lives there, but
it must be haunted by many ghosts. In 1581, alarmed by Drake's passage in 1578, Spain launched an expedition with the object of fortifying
the Straits and so preventing or discouraging any similar exploit. More
than two years after the start of what was to be a most ill-fated venture,
the Spanish fleet entered the Straits. But before they had even reached
the First Narrows, one of the ships was cast ashore. A party of four hundred men and thirty women were landed to salvage the stores. Leaving
this party in charge of a Lieutenant Viedma, Sarmiento with a hundred
men marched westward along the coast to this Santa Ana point, while
a pinnace with stores followed by sea. A fort and a settlement were
built and the place named Ciudad del Rey Felipe. On the approach
of winter Sarmiento tried to unite his two garrisons, but bad weather
drove his ship out of the Straits. Undaunted, he made two unsuccessful attempts in two different ships to succour his starving countrymen.
Viedma, having come to the end of his resources, marched overland to
Rey Felipe, a move which probably only hastened the doom of both
settlements. By the end of the second winter only fifteen men and three
women remained alive.

In 1587 Cavendish, on the third circumnavigation of the globe,
anchored at Rey Felipe, changing its name to Port Famine. He found
there a fort with four cannon and 'several churches'. Of the people
who once worshipped there, we are told: 'At last they died like so many
dogs, in their houses, in great numbers; and the stench of these putri-
fying carcasses infecting those that survived they were forced to quit
the town with one consent, and go rambling upon the sea coasts living
upon roots and leaves and sea herbs, or what animals they at any time
happily caught'. It was this tragic story of Rey Felipe which probably gave rise to the legend that there was a lost city somewhere in the
mountains far to the north of the Straits, a city founded by the rem-
nants of Sarmiento's hapless garrison.

In the morning, there being no wind, we started motoring in order
to round Cape Froward. The glass was falling, the western sky looked

dirty, and we had no wish to be caught in a gale from ahead off this noto-riously stormy cape. We had with us no Belloc whose love for the sea and sail was equalled only by his hatred of machinery. 'I would rather die of thirst', he writes, 'ten miles off the headland in a brazen calm, than have on board what is monstrously called an auxiliary... For it is with head-lands as with harbours, if you have machinery aboard your craft is gone.' Whether it is done under sail or power, the rounding of a great cape, more especially a cape that divides two oceans, has about it something both solemn and elating. Although it is a normal and long foreseen step, the moment the cape looms in sight the pent-up hopes and fears of a long voyage focus themselves upon its successful rounding.

Cape Froward is not like Cape Horn. The rounding of it, unlike that of its more famous and tempestuous neighbour, confers none of the traditional privileges such as spitting to windward or drinking the loyal toast with one foot on the table. Nevertheless, it is a noble and impressive headland, in shape and size not unlike the Horn. Both capes are of much the same height, the one 1200 ft. and the other 1300 ft., and in pictures their profiles are alike. Each springs boldly from the sea to a sort of step before it rises steeply to a summit which is frequently snow-covered. To the west of Cape Froward the climate suddenly changes and becomes both wetter and windier. That a change for the worse is at hand is often foretold by a violent storm off the cape itself. As the *South America Pilot* says: 'The change in the vicinity of the cape is often very striking. The squalls are exceptionally heavy, the weather frequently changes to heavy rain or snow, and the shores will often be invisible.' A sailing vessel bound west round the Horn, upon reaching the pitch of the Cape would not notice any such sudden change; for the weather would no doubt be just as vile throughout Drake Sea or Strait, that 500-mile stretch of stormy, open water between Cape Horn and the South Shetlands.

Equally remarkable, too, is the change of scene as one moves from the east to the western part of the Straits. Just as on land the traveller from the east ascends from the flat pampas through foothills to the Cordillera, so by sea he makes a 'voyage through the Andes'. In his book *South America* Lord Bryce describes the change thus:

Rounding Cape Froward: The white cross on the summit can be distinguished; at the foot of the cape and beyond it, part of the snow-covered Darwin range on Tierra del Fuego can be seen

Magellan's Straits are unlike any other straits in this respect, that the physical aspect of the two ends is entirely different. The character of the shores on each side is the same in each part, but both shores of the eastern half, from the Atlantic to Cape Froward, are unlike those of the western half from Cape Froward to the Pacific. The former has low banks with smooth outlines, slopes of earth or sand dipping into shallow water, and a climate extremely dry. The latter half is enclosed between high, steep mountains which are drenched by incessant rains. The eastern half is a channel leading through the southernmost part of the Argentine plain, which has apparently been raised from the sea bottom in comparatively recent times. The western half is a deep narrow cut through the extremity of a great mountain system that stretches north for thousands of miles, forming the western edge of S. America, and the rocks on each side of it are ancient. The western half is grand and solemn, with its deep waters mirroring white crags and blue glaciers. The low eastern half has no beauty save that which belongs to vast open spaces of level land and smooth water over which broods the silence of a clear and lucent air. A more singular contrast, all within a few hours steaming, it would be hard to find.

Having got fairly up to this defiant-looking headland we stopped the engine and sailed slowly past with a light northwesterly breeze, passing near enough to see clearly the big white cross on the summit. The wind then freshening from dead ahead we sought shelter in the attractively named Snug Bay, about five miles north-west of the cape. The bay belied its name, for it is wide open to the west and it was to that quarter that the wind was backing. While lunching below we paid frequent visits on deck to see if the anchor was dragging. It is the kind of place of which the *Pilot* elsewhere advises the mariner that 'anchoring in this bight must be prompted by necessity and not by any hope of tranquillity'.

So far from tranquil were we that at 2 o'clock, in a rising wind and sea, we got up our anchor and sailed out. As Froward Reach is amply wide enough for manoeuvre we began to beat against wind, sea, and driving rain, for using the engine in such conditions was merely a waste of petrol. We sailed in this way all through the night, for although the reach is unlit there are no dangers and the iron-bound shores are steep-to. By daybreak we were off Pond Sound on the southern side and more than ready to seek shelter after such a wet, cold and anxious night. The necessity of putting the ship about at irregular and frequent intervals had meant that two of us had continually to be on deck, one steering and the other standing by. It was becoming clear that if the conditions met with on this first day and night west of Cape Froward were usual (as they were) a tough time lay ahead of us. The entrance to Pond Sound looked intricate and as we had not yet accustomed our weak nerves to threading tortuous passages beset with rocks, mostly within the proverbial biscuit's toss, we plumped for Port Gallant. This was reputedly one of the best anchorages in the Straits, spacious, sheltered, easy of access, and of moderate depth. Most often the depth is immoderate—a factor which rules out many otherwise safe and charming little holes where the mariner could hope to enjoy a care-free night. 'No bottom at ten fathoms' was too frequently the leadsman's cry, and if one despaired of finding a better hole and went in close, by the time the anchor was dropped in eight fathoms one found oneself within spitting distance of the shore, the ship having no room to swing.

Throughout the day the weather worsened and we were thankful when we reached the shelter of Fortescue Bay and anchored in Port Gallant at its head. Since leaving Snug Bay, more than twenty-four hours earlier, we had made good about 20 miles. When Slocum passed this way in 1896 he was pursued by savages from Fortescue Bay. In 1908 Skottsberg, too, met Indians, one of whom, Mrs Ahichakwarrakwilties (Mission name, Emilia) came on board his steamer. Accordingly our hopes of seeing some of these uncouth people ran high, but, alas, we found there only a naval tanker, the *Maipu*, at anchor with a boat's crew ashore gathering mussels.

In one way we were not sorry to see her, for I had just discovered that as a result of some bad mathematics we had not enough paraffin for cooking to last three months. As our anchor went down the *Maipu* recalled her boat and started to weigh. Hastily we launched our dinghy and got alongside just as she began to move. She carried no paraffin. Barely had the dinghy got back with this bad news when the two cruisers which we had seen at Punta Arenas steamed into the bay and anchored half a mile away. Surely a cruiser would carry a Primus stove as a sort of secondary armament, as it were, a spare *batterie de cuisine* should the electric stove fail? Hunger, or the threatened paraffin shortage with all its implications, made us bold. After consulting the International Code, we hoisted the signal, 'I am in need of paraffin'. At Punta Arenas the good will of the navy toward us had made so deep and lasting an impression that I think we half expected the admiral—if there was one on board—to come over in his barge towing a 40-gal. drum of paraffin. Nothing happened. One of the cruisers made a signal which we could not read and which was probably meant for her con-sort or the disappearing tanker, so we determined to visit them early next morning.

On a falsely bright morning, after a night of wind and rain, Michael and Jorge rowed to the cruisers which lay well down wind of *Mischief*. After a long pull they got alongside first one and then the other, their stay in each case being so short that we could only con-clude that their mission had failed. As they began the long plug back against the wind it began to blow harder, and through our glasses we watched their desperately slow progress with growing concern. Finally, we weighed anchor and motored down to them. Having picked them up we anchored again while we stowed the dinghy and made ready for sea. We beat out of the bay in a driving snow storm—the weather changes quickly in those parts—dipping our ensign to the cruisers. They, having more sense, remained at anchor.

Although it was late spring both the scene and the weather were wintry. The rain of the preceding night, falling as snow upon the grey hills around the bay, had clothed them with white to within five hundred feet of the sea; and as *Mischief* left the shelter of the bay to begin beating westward along English Reach she was assailed by furious squalls of rain, sleet, and snow. The squalls were prolonged, the intervals between them brief. But in these well-nigh land-locked channels there is never any sea to throw a boat about and *Mischief* was stiff and stout enough to sail happily in all but the strongest blasts under storm jib, reefed staysail, and reefed mainsail. In these waters this became our normal rig and we seldom had occasion to alter it. We had hoped to make Tilly Bay, but after one of our hard-est day's sailing, wind and tide defeated us. English Reach, the con-tinuation of Froward Reach, is divided into two narrow channels by the Charles Islands which lie in mid-stream, so that the tides run

strongly. Late in the afternoon, when the tide turned against us, we
started the engine to help the sails. It was no good. Although at the
start of a fresh tack we might be pointing at a mark on the far shore
a good mile further west, inexorably the tide set us back. We barely
held our ground, so after wasting much precious petrol on this tread-
mill we turned and ran back to Mussel Bay where we anchored in
five fathoms some fifty yards from the mouth of a small stream. We
had made good only ten miles. For a long day's beating against wind
and rain, a discipline to which we had now become resigned, it was
a small reward. Yet it was fascinating sailing; rounding miniature
capes, peeping into hidden coves, tacking between rocky wooded
shores backed by sombre fells of yellow heath and grey slabs, and
over all the low, driving clouds. Desolate and forsaken as the scene
was, it had the powerful appeal of an untrodden land and the bracing challenge of unsparing harshness.

Early next morning everyone went ashore to collect firewood,
mussels, and flowers. As it was our first landing on this wild coast
we experienced a most satisfying thrill. As we ranged along the shore
and a little way inland through bush and swamp, remarking the trees,
the plants, the birds, a lake, and finally the mournful framework of
a rude hut, we did indeed recapture something of 'those first experiences, and felt as earlier men felt in a happier time'. Firewood was
needed for the cabin stove, now most necessary; the mussels of these
coasts are famous for their size and succulence; while by collecting
flowers I hoped to pay my modest tribute to science. From its rectangular shape we judged the hut to have been once the temporary
home of some seal or sea otter hunter and not that of Canoe Indians
whose wigwams were merely poles and withies bent together. The
land birds were few and small, like wrens, but on a rock by the shore
was a solitary kelp goose. The gander is snow white and in these parts
may often be seen, a solitary white figure on some rocky point. The
browny black plumage of the female so matches the colour of the surroundings that only a closer inspection will show her standing alongside her mate. A starving man might eat a kelp goose readily, but
Brillat-Savarin himself would despair of making from it a dish fit for
a gastronome. Placed somewhere between these extremes, we ate this
one without enthusiasm, but out of consideration for the marksman

we held our comment. Long use and wont might reconcile one to their fishy taste, but these birds are too wary to figure frequently on one's menu.

We sailed out as soon as the flood tide began to make. There was the usual head wind but the strong tide took us up to Crosstide Cape in three hours. Hereabouts three tidal streams meet—by English Reach from the Atlantic, by Crooked Reach from the Pacific, and by Canal Jerome from the miniature inland sea of Otway Water. Off the cape the wind died down and we had to start the engine to reach our chosen anchorage in Butler Bay. According to the *Pilot* 'for small vessels with local knowledge Butler Bay affords anchorage on its western side over a bottom of rock more or less covered with mud'. Even without local knowledge the information was enough. We were always amazed by the thoroughness of the sailing directions, for they were based largely on surveys by sailing vessels over a hundred years ago. The names of men like Fitzroy, Stokes, Lecky, Wharton, and their ships, *Beagle*, *Adventure*, *Sylvia*, *Nassau*, recur constantly on the charts. We were humbled by the thoughts of those men who had spent so many years in these tempestuous waters, hemmed in among islets and hidden rocks, riding out gales, drenched by constant rain, and who in open boats sought out and sounded all the various channels and anchorages.

In the evening after a day of rain and sleet, we dropped anchor in 4 fathoms only about twenty yards from shore. Butler Bay is not on the mainland but on Santa Ines island on the south-west side of the Straits. It is a large island with a range of snow peaks and many glaciers, all unexplored. As an example of the troubles that may beset climbing parties in these regions it is worth mentioning briefly a recent attempt to traverse Santa Ines from east to west as described by Saint Loup in *Monts Pacifique*. As an introduction the party and its equipment were flooded out of their first camp on the beach by an exceptionally high tide. Having climbed about 2500 ft. over rock and wet snow they reached the foot of a glacier where they established a camp. Ahead they could see a sort of ice basin surrounded by formidable peaks. A blizzard in the night, with wind up to 80mph wrecked their sodden tents and so discouraged them that after drinking half a litre of brandy each they came down. This

last domestic detail calls to mind one of the early attempts on Mont
Blanc, but in that case the party suffered from lassitude which they
found 'could not be conquered without the aid of liquor'. But no
doubt the weather on these outer islands, which receive the first
unbroken fury of the Pacific gales, is worse than any we experienced
on the ice-cap itself.

For supper that night we had the mussels gathered at Mussel Bay.
This bay is by no means remarkable for mussels, which abound every-
where. It was so named by Cavendish: 'We put into a cove on the south
side which we called Muskle Cove because there were great store of
them.' Mussels were the main food of the Canoe Indians. In most bays
and coves are still to be found middens or heaps of discarded shells
which mark the sites of their most favoured encampments. Dr Junius
Bird of the American Natural History Museum, who has made a study
of the culture of the original inhabitants of these coasts, has excavated
middens in the Beagle Channel region which were thirteen feet deep.
He points out three things that did a little to mitigate the harshness of
life in the channels—things, rather, which made life possible for people
who had no clothes other than a patch of seal-skin and no shelter other
than the rudest wigwam of branches and leaves. First there was the
'tepu' tree (*Tepualis stipularis*). This can be cut and burnt when green,
and even in heavy rain a fire can be coaxed from its fine twigs. Then the
Antarctic beech which provided bark with which to make canoes, and
thirdly mussels. These provided not only a freely available food but
also an essential tool, for from the shell of the giant 'chorro' they made
an effective knife.

Darwin, who met numbers of these Indians in the Beagle Channel,
thought them less than admirable:

These Fuegians were the most abject and miserable creatures I anywhere beheld. They were quite naked and one full grown woman was
absolutely so. It was raining heavily, and the fresh water, together
with the spray, trickled down her body. These poor wretches were
stunted in their growth, their hideous faces bedaubed, their skins
filthy and greasy, their hair entangled, their voices discordant, and
their gestures violent. Viewing such men one could hardly make oneself believe that they are fellow creatures and inhabitants of the same

world. It is a common subject of conjecture what pleasures in life some of the lower animals can enjoy; how much more reasonably the same question may be asked with respect to these barbarians.

Brutish though they were—a picture in Skottsberg's book shows two who look as if they had that moment come down from their tree—any man who has in more favoured regions tried 'living on the country' cannot but feel respect for a race so intrinsically tough that they could hold their own in so inhospitable a country. Darwin goes on:

> Their skill, like the instinct of animals, is not improved by experience; their canoe, their most ingenious work poor as it may be, has remained the same for the last three hundred years. Although essentially the same creature how little must the mind of one of these beings resemble that of an educated man. What a scale of improvement is comprehended between the faculties of a Fuegian savage and a Sir Isaac Newton! Whence have these people come? What could have tempted a tribe of men leaving the fine regions of the north to travel down the Cordillera, to invent and build canoes, and then to enter one of the most inhospitable countries of the world?

Without canoes, of course, these people could not have reached these coasts, for there is no way by land. One can only presume that they were driven there by fear. In the Patagonian channels they were at any rate unmolested. Provided they could survive unclad in the constant rain and cold, and had the skill and the material to build canoes so that they could move from one mussel bed to another—for all movement overland was impossible—they had nothing to fear. Nothing to fear that is, until the coming of their so-called betters; the sailors, sealers, and traders who traded drink for skins; and the missionaries who killed by misguided zeal and ill-directed kindness. As Mark Twain said: 'Soap and education are not so sudden as a massacre, but they are more deadly in the long run.'

'Mussels for supper and snow after' is the last enigmatic entry in my note of Butler Bay. The following day, 1 December, we suffered a serious mishap. On a dry, dull morning we motored out and as there was no wind outside we kept the engine running. Two hours later a valve spring broke. The box of spare parts made up for us by the agents for our type of engine had no replacement. The engine could not be used except for short spells in moments of crisis or when making or leaving harbour. Peel Inlet looked an uncommonly long way off.

Meantime a fair wind sprang up. With some help from the tide it took us quickly to Field anchorage. While we were considering what we should now do, for the wind had dropped, we saw our first glacier at close quarters. This was a lovely stream of ice tumbling down from a 4000 ft. peak and ending in a sheer drop to the water's edge. But our course was decided for us, for the wind began to blow strongly from north-west and now that we had no engine we could not afford to waste any wind. We had to push on another five miles to Playa Prada. In the increasing wind accompanied by torrential rain and sleet we gained the shelter of the outer anchorage and turned on the engine to negotiate the extremely narrow pass to the inner one. We passed within a few yards of a wall of rock as straight and smooth as a dockside.

The inner anchorage is a most beautiful cirque of rock and these enclosing walls are thickly covered with trees and ferns. The hanging valley just discernible above the cirque evidently contains a glacier, for two cataracts of water spilt over the wall while yet a third stream had cut back into the rock to form a deep cleft. Save for the roar of the falls the place was profoundly still. Overhead and outside in the reach a gale raged. Curtains of rain swept ceaselessly across the cirque but not a ripple disturbed the steel grey water of the anchorage. Many of these apparently sheltered anchorages are blasted at times by 'williwaws'; in fact, at Playa Prada, according to the *Pilot*, williwaws occasionally blow from all directions with great force. These squalls blow down almost vertically from high ground with appalling fury and are particularly met with near the foot of a valley or below a break in the hills. They are not confined to enclosed anchorages—indeed in such places we were never disturbed—and when sailing close to a steep shore or even in the middle of a narrow channel a ship may be struck and perhaps thrown on its beam ends.

While the rain fell in great gouts we sat below in moderate comfort with a smart fire burning. As is a habit of cabin skylights ours leaked a little so that throughout our stay in the channels we had to keep the cover on. The canvas having been waterproofed with a preparation of my own making had a yellowish glaze, and the subdued light reminded us of sitting in an aquarium. It was not only the light that gave us this idea for most things about us were wet. The twilight of the cabin reflected our drooping spirits. We had expected bad weather but not quite so bad as that which we were now experiencing. Rain, bitter squalls of hail and snow, strong winds funnelling their way down the channels from dead ahead, were our daily and nightly portion. Perhaps we deserved it, for it resembled the Punishment of Gluttons in the Inferno:

> Ceaseless, accursed, heavy and cold, unchanged
> For ever both in kind and in degree:
> Large hail, discoloured water, sleety flaw,
> Through the dim midnight air streamed down amain.

We had scarcely seen the sun since leaving Punta Arenas and the glass now stood at 28.75, well below the normal for that region. The breakdown of the engine also weighed heavily on us, and since it could not be repaired our 80 gal. of petrol on deck and the prospect of more at Puerto Bueno merely added to our exasperation. Equally worrying was the paraffin shortage. We had already begun to economise and those left on board at Peel Inlet would have to make do with wood. An almost painless method of economising had been devised by John in the form of what he called dual purpose pie. One must imagine a beef steak and kidney pudding (bully beef doing duty for both steak and kidney) crowned with a 6-in. thick roof of pastry. One ate half the roof with the meat and put the remainder aside to eat later with jam or treacle as the sweet. Since all ills are good when attended by food, we ate one that night.

CHAPTER VIII

INTO THE CHANNELS

◆

The general features of these channels are high, abrupt shores, with innumerable peaks; their bold rugged heads giving an appearance of gloomy grandeur rarely seen elsewhere. In proceeding through them the general rule should be to keep in mid-channel and avoid all kelp.

SOUTH AMERICA PILOT

IT HAD RAINED ALL NIGHT and now it only ceased for a short time as we weighed anchor and motored out into Long Reach. Fifteen minutes was the maximum time we were allowed to use the engine, and John, who had charge of it, was becoming increasingly reluctant to use it at all for fear of making bad worse. In heavy rain and squalls we tacked back and forth across the reach. At 4 o'clock, when we had made good some seven miles, we seemed to be losing ground. We therefore had to decide whether to make for a cove on the south side with the discouraging name of Rocky Inlet, or Marion Cove on the north. The *Pilot* had merely told us that the entrance to Rocky Inlet was fringed with kelp, but that the depths in Marion cove were so great that even a small vessel anchored in twenty-five fathoms would be unable to veer enough cable to swing. To Rocky Inlet therefore we went, sounding our way cautiously. It too was deep, but we found bottom among kelp some thirty yards from the shore.

Charles, having in his time learnt the nautical patter for sounding, usually undertook the cold, wet task of swinging the lead. His sonorous cries, 'by the deep six', 'and a half six', 'by the mark seven', or more often, 'no bottom at fifteen', enthralled us and mystified Jorge who, until we enlightened him, apparently mistook 'no bottom' for the equally depressing cry of 'no bottle'. The kelp which surrounded us is a characteristic feature of these waters. 'Keep clear of kelp' had been the reiterated advice of the old salts at Punta Arenas. Certainly, when under way one should not ignore it, for kelp implies rocks. On almost every rock, from low water mark down to very great depths, the weed grows in long streamers. Captain Fitzroy found it growing up from a rock at a depth of forty-five fathoms. Since it does not grow directly upwards but lies at an acute angle, it can attain a very great length. Captain Cook, who met with it at the Kerguelens—for it is very widespread— affirmed that 360 ft. was no uncommon length. Kelp, therefore, may often be seen on the surface in deep water, while the rock from which it streams may be close to the surface and a hundred yards away. If the tide is strong the kelp that is seen is often far from its parent rock, or the current may be strong enough to run it under so that it is not seen at all. The Pilot quotes an instance of the danger which may lurk in kelp beds: one of the *Beagle*'s boats having sounded a large bed of kelp and considering it might be safely crossed, found a rock not more than four feet in diameter and only six feet below the surface. Besides thus buoying hidden dangers, kelp makes an excellent breakwater behind which a small boat can find smooth water. Sealers, Canoe Indians, and such like, used to moor their boats with a piece of growing kelp and lie to it as securely as at anchor. Slocum himself, in Crooked Reach, when the wind had died, moored Spray by kelp in twenty fathoms and held her there for several hours against a three-knot current.

We spent another idle evening in Rocky Inlet, for the rain was such that we could neither go ashore nor carry out the much needed repairs to sheets and sails. The everlasting going-about had caused more wear and tear than a long ocean passage, and the sodden state of sheets and sails had made them more susceptible to chafe and had delayed the necessary repair. It is little use stitching wet canvas or trying to splice a sodden rope. That night for the first time we set an anchor watch; it was very squally and *Mischief* when swinging seemed to us too anxious to nuzzle some nearby rocks.

With the glass rising we expected better times. It was now very cold. The snow which fell during the night did not confine itself to the high ground but covered *Mischief*'s deck as well. In the morning the wind was fair and in spite of frequent squalls of snow or hail gave us a grand day's sailing. Instead of beating to and fro across the channel we could now lay a course nearly parallel to the shores which slid past as they had never done before. Further west the scene becomes even more desolate, a succession of low rounded hills, and hummocks of white granite, bald as granite setts. This absence of vegetation was owing mainly to the slate giving place to granite, but the greater exposure to Pacific gales no doubt played a part. By now Long Reach had merged into Sea Reach and we were on the threshold of the great ocean whose throb and heave we soon began to feel. We sped past Cripples Channel. Ahead of us Cape Tamar, round which we had to pass to reach the Patagonian channels, reared its great bulk. On our port hand lay Desolation island, thus named by Sir John Narborough 'because it is so desolate a land to behold'.

Cape Tamar is a critical point for small vessels bound for the Patagonian channels, for the twelve miles of water which must be traversed before the sheltered water of Smyth channel is reached are exposed to the full sweep of the Pacific. Fortunately the conditions under which we were to approach it could scarce be bettered. Since leaving Rocky Inlet we had tacked only once, and rounding Cape Tamar we should bring the wind on our quarter. Soon the two peaks on Tamar Island showed above the cape and Rhoda Pass opened to starboard. This pass is a narrow channel between the island and Tamar peninsular on which the cape lies. It is used by small vessels to avoid the heavy seas usually met with off the island. Since this pass has at one point a width of less than a cable, and as we were under sail, we thought it best to go outside, heavy seas notwithstanding. At 7 o'clock we had the island abeam and having made a good offing squared away for the entrance to Smyth channel. The sea was rough but by no means heavy. Westwards towards the open ocean lay a magnificently stern and wild seascape. To the south stretched the black and fiercely serrated skyline of Desolation Island, terminating far to the west in the unmistakable profile of Cape Pillar, one of the two western guardians of the Straits. Dark storm clouds passed in procession over the savage peaks of Desolation, while from the direction of Pillar a drifting white curtain—a white squall—marched with gathering speed towards us. Even were there no squall in the offing the Evangelistas, the notorious rocks which form the other guardian of the Straits, lying fifteen miles north-west of Cape Pillar, would have been hardly visible. The relief of the men who man the Evangelistas lighthouse is a difficult and dangerous task. Winds of

Off Cape Tamar near the western end of the Straits; the cape is on an island and between it and the Tamar peninsula, which can be seen behind, is the Rhoda Pass, a channel used by small vessels; the so-called 'graveyard of ships', where a number of wrecks lie, is on the extreme left

Mischief anchored in Wodehouse Bay in Canal Sarmiento; the mast looks stumpy as it is without the topmast

force eight or above are reached on about eighty days of the year at the western entrance to the Straits.* An anchorage on one of the nearby islands is called Cuarenta Dias, reputedly because a relief ship once waited there for forty days before being able to effect a landing. At Punta Arenas, Lieutenant Hudson told us that recently his ship had had to wait thirty days before the relief could be carried out.

In these waters the rule never to waste a fair wind applies with singular force. In the ten hours since leaving Rocky Inlet we had covered nearly fifty miles. As this was the equivalent of three or four days of beating against head winds we decided to carry on throughout the night. Smyth channel is by no means plain sailing. It has a sharp bend, small capes project from the shores and small islets lie off them; but there is a lighthouse on Fairway Islets at the entrance and three unmanned lights mark the principal dangers beyond. Fairway is the only manned light in the channels before reaching Tarn Bay at the northern exit from the channels into the Gulf of Peñas. It was necessary to go carefully, and as a warning and a reminder we had on our starboard hand a group of reefs known as the 'Stragglers' where we could distinguish the gaunt, twisted ironwork of several wrecks. There was no response when we reported our name by lamp to the Fairway lighthouse, and soon after the light, as well as the shores of Smyth channel, vanished from our sight in a heavy squall of rain. With a promontory thrusting out into the channel ahead of us and some islets beyond, we were profoundly relieved when the rain began to thin. Soon it was clear enough for us to make out the light on the promontory, but when the next light came in sight, that on Shoal Island, a new peril arose. The wind died, and to avoid being set on the island, for the tide was running strongly, we had recourse to our lame engine. This calm stayed with us until dawn when a strongish wind from ahead obliged us to begin beating again. By midday we reached our chosen anchorage in Otter Bay where a wood and mussel party immediately went off. I stayed aboard to repair the staysail which for the first time for many days was dry, and having done that I joined the foraging

---

* The comparative figure for the western entrance to the English Channel is thirty-two days. Further east off the Needles it is only twenty-five.

party on shore. When Charles met me there I took him for Robinson Crusoe, a little down-at-heels.

Though the Otter islands are well wooded they are, like many other parts of the channels, remarkably bare of life. Cormorants are the commonest birds but small numbers of ducks, penguins, and kelp geese frequent the shore. In the nearby woods small creeper wrens, finches, kingfishers, and thrushes may be met with, but nowhere in any number. Although it was early summer neither the song nor the twittering of birds was much heard, and one could well believe that the merriest songster might be subdued by the gloomy solemnity of its surroundings. Indeed, under a thick canopy of both living and decaying trees, dripping with moisture and draped in moss, where the rare shafts of sunlight scarce can penetrate, man himself is oppressed into silence.

The sea-birds, too, went about their affairs quietly. We seldom heard the braying or mooing of penguins, and the steamer ducks only became really noisy when beating the water in frantic flight. This species of duck which cannot fly was given the name 'Racehorse duck' by the men of the shipwrecked *Wager*, one of Lord Anson's squadron, because of the speed at which it travelled. Captain Stokes, who commanded the *Beagle* on her first commission in these waters in 1826–8, preferred to call them steamer duck after the paddle steamers then coming more and more into use. The local name *patos vapor* is merely a literal translation of the English. Their wings are too small and weak for flight but they scuttle over the water at an astonishing pace half swimming and half running, flapping the water with their wings and making so much splash and fuss about it all that the whole business is extremely comical. We never tired of watching them. On the approach of the strange sea monster *Mischief* they would begin swimming in uncertain circles. Then, becoming a little more agitated, the whole party would gather together and increase speed on what was thought to be a safe course. Faster and faster they went until at last the retreat became a rout when with one accord the whole flock broke into frenzied flight, wings and legs going like pistons, each bird half lost in a cloud of spray. When really worked up their estimated speed is from fifteen to twenty knots. Darwin's opinion that their wings move alternately like the legs is disputed. But because of the amount of spray they throw up and the speed at which they move, this weighty problem is not so easily solved.

Amusement is all these creatures provide. For although with cunning, perseverance, and a high velocity rifle they can be killed they can hardly be eaten, for the meat is tough, oily, and fishy. Small shot, even buckshot, rattles off them harmlessly, and Darwin records his failure to break a steamer duck's skull with a geological hammer! After cormorants they were the birds most commonly seen and, since they weigh as much as twenty to thirty pounds, it annoyed us to find them such impossible table birds. It is generally true that where any particular herb grows there lives the ass who is to eat it, and no doubt an all-wise Providence provided steamer ducks for the strong stomachs of Canoe Indians and shipwrecked mariners. The fact that we could not stomach, much less relish them (Procter's disapproval was not very severe), seemed to me to betray our inadequacy as travellers; for proverbially a traveller must have the back of an ass to bear all and the mouth of a hog to eat what is set before him.

The entries in the log were becoming a little monotonous. 'Fresh wind from ahead, increasing later, rain most of the day', was again recorded for the next day. But we made good some 15 miles, coming to rest in the evening in Isthmus Bay, a good anchorage on the east side of the channel where we found two broken huts. Mount Burney, 5800 ft. high, always snow covered and only a few miles from the coast, had remained hidden all day.

Michael and I went plant-hunting, and thanks to the forest having at one time been cleared we were able to penetrate half a mile inland, discovering on the way berberis, fuschia, a fine scarlet-flowered shrub, and strangely enough the remains of a fence. What had induced anyone, we wondered, to settle here to farm, and how long had it been before this courageous or crazy settler retired discomfited? Where the forest had been cleared nothing now grew but moss and a few scattered tussocks of coarse grass. The absence of feed explained the fence, for no sheep would consent to remain there tethered only by his teeth; and, unless the settler himself was as self-sufficient as a Canoe Indian, he would not be able to maintain life and would depend upon supplies from Punta Arenas. It is most unlikely that this long stretch of coast and its innumerable islands will ever be settled.

To describe it in the Whitehall farmer's phrase as 'marginal land' would be a euphemism as extravagant as Lord Salisbury's well known description of the Sahara as 'very light soil'. This labyrinth of channels and islands seems to be useless to man. Where the shores are not of bare rock they are covered with scrubby evergreen forest which, a thousand feet above, peters out into boggy moor, rock, and ice. And this whole bleak landscape is swept, summer and winter alike, by high winds and persistent rain.

With more zeal than prudence, the barometer falling steadily, we sailed out next morning hoping to get though Victory Pass into Canal Sarmiento. By noon our hopes had vanished. Squall followed squall until our lee rail, three feet above the deck, was awash. In the afternoon these williwaws, for such they were, continued striking us from all directions with great violence; and while we were reefing the mainsail still more closely we were twice taken aback. On all sides the water was being whipped up into the air, giving the channel the appearance of a rough plain swept by dust-devils. Any port in a storm. Our nearest refuge was Inlet Bay, referred to briefly in the Pilot as 'for small vessels with local knowledge'; and having fought our way well to windward we turned and ran in. The noises emitted by our suffering engine had become so strange that we dared not use it. So that when entering this small, kelp-strewn cove under sail alone the faces of the crew grew more and more troubled. Until the anchor was down and the sails off we looked, in the words of Uncle Remus, 'like every minit wuz gwineter be de nex'.

Next day as we beat up to the entrance to Victory Pass the sun came out, the wind backed, and with a fair wind we sailed merrily through. Gloomy grandeur is a just description of the scenery of the channels, but how swiftly does a touch of sunlight dispel the gloom. How fair then can be the scene when in bright sun and pearly clear air the lichen covered rocks glow with the rich warmth of an old stone wall, the granite outcrops sparkle, and the flat grey of the fells breaks into light and shade, a patchwork of green and yellow with purple cloud shadows drifting across.

Victory Pass leading into Collingwood Strait at the south end of Canal Sarmiento runs at right angles to the general north and south trend of the channels. With a following wind here one might fairly expect a beam wind in Collingwood Strait. In the channels, however, one hardly ever enjoys a beam wind; for no matter from what direction, the wind is funnelled up or down the reach, so that a vessel always finds it either from ahead or astern. When, therefore, we found ourselves once more beating after having turned the corner into Collingwood Strait, we felt more hurt than surprised. Attracted by the name we had intended to make the Bay of Islands, but when the wind increased we turned into Columbine Cove on the western shore, having done only thirteen miles. In more ways than one it was a lucky decision. Rowing ashore I spotted several duck (or geese?) behind a little spit. Putting back hastily I brought John off armed with our .22 rifle. After a short stalk he killed two. These handsome birds had bronze necks and backs, with white wings shading to green at the tips; and after due hanging they provided a memorable meal.

In the channels a day seldom passed without our sighting a steamer. Generally these were small tankers or coasters, Chilean, Norwegian, Danish, and German. We learnt later that a German boat in which our friend Gird Breuer was travelling to Valparaiso, dropped a tin container of mail for us to pick up. As we had no inkling of her intention, and as she was steaming at twelve knots half a mile away, it was a singularly careless and unsuccessful way of delivering mail. None of these ships showed any interest in us and we had not thought it worth making an effort to stop one to ask about valve springs. At sundown, however, another ship passed which we recognised as our former acquaintance the *Maipu*. When she slowed down and began to turn towards the cove we became excited. A quarter mile out she stopped, her cable ran out, and before the roar had died away Jorge and I were halfway to her in the dinghy.

As we came alongside and climbed the Jacob's ladder the steel sides of this small ship appeared to us quite vast. With friendly grins we were ushered to the captain's cabin. A bell was pressed and a steward brought beer. Another bell summoned the chief engineer who having learnt our need went through his stores and ultimately found a spring of approximately the right size. With this treasure, a sack of bread, potatoes, and some tinned food we returned to *Mischief* while the *Maipu* began to shorten her cable. Nor was the matter of paraffin forgotten. While we were there the captain had a signal sent off asking

that some should be sent with the petrol to Puerto Bueno. His only
request had been for a picture of *Mischief*. So back went the dinghy
with the best photograph we had. Whereupon the *Maipu*, with a fare-
well blast, steamed out of the cove.

From Columbine Cove our way lay through the narrow Farquar
Pass at the north end of Newton island into Canal Sarmiento. Conditions were better that day, the head wind was less violent and by noon
the rain had stopped. Anxious to begin work on the engine we put into
Wodehouse Bay on Piazzi island on the west side of the channel, where
a wreck to the north of the entrance provides easy identification. Many
of these bays and coves are not so readily identified. Sometimes they
are not even seen as the entrance may not open up until one has sailed
past it, or it may appear so insignificant that it is just disregarded. It is
always important in coastal sailing, and particularly so here, to identify
everything in sight and to know at all times where one is.

We had made good some fifteen miles. Leaving John and Charles
to begin work on the engine the rest of us went ashore to gather mussels and cook them on a wood fire. Wodehouse Bay is another lovely
anchorage. Indeed all these lonely little bays are endowed with a wild
beauty. The wildness and loneliness is intensified by storm and the
beauty only reaches its full bloom under a benign sky. The bay seemed
devoid of life. The channel being out of sight, *Mischief* lay as if in a
landlocked pool nodding very gently to her reflection in the water. In
the far distance stretched the long, jagged line of the Sarmiento Cordillera, the higher snow-covered peaks glowing faintly pink in the setting sun, while further to the north two bold spires of rock and ice
marked the extreme southern end of the ice-cap.

For six solid hours our two engineers John and Charles (the one
supplying the practice and the other the theory) battled to extract the
broken spring. Armed as they were with little better than their bare
hands—for we had no valve-lifter—it was an unequal contest. Lying
in my bunk watching the struggle through the cabin doorway, while
our black gang became rapidly blacker, I had leisure to reflect upon
how pleasant it is to see a battle from a distant hill. At intervals they
would withdraw into the cabin to cool off and to draw diagrams on the
once-white table explanatory of the various conceivable ways in which
a valve spring could be fitted. Having eliminated by trial and error the

two most likely ways, our theorist now voiced his considered opinion, based on what he had heard of the American way of life and their readiness to scrap the outmoded or outworn, that the valves of this American engine were not removable, and that if a spring did break the engine should be incontinently scrapped. This led to a heated exchange, more personal than mechanical, until at last they decided to sleep on it.

Morning brought enlightenment for in a short time they found what had before escaped them, two small, hardly visible collars holding down the valve. Soon it was out. Then, with much ingenuity, a hand vice, pieces of cord, and some strong language they compressed the new spring, fitted it, and by midday the engine was running. In heavy rain we motored out but on meeting a very strong wind we put back, having at last concluded that the wear and tear on the gear when beating against these winds was not worth the few miles gained. When the weather cleared in the evening we were not tempted out. Instead we bathed and washed clothes in a fresh water pool, leaving John to cook the Columbine cove duck over a wood fire. Very good it proved, too, with no fishy taint whatever.

By morning (Saturday, 10 December, a fortnight out from Punta Arenas) the weather had again deteriorated; but after lunch, when the barometer rose a little, we ventured out. We should have done better to stay where we were. After seven hours of beating, with everything reefed down, we made good six miles The tide turned against us, and we were thankful to reach Occasion Cove late in the evening. It had been a beast of a day. Occasion Cove (Caleta Occasion) is at the back of a bigger bay called Lecky Retreat. Captain S. T. S. Lecky is better known as the author of *Lecky's Wrinkles in Practical Navigation*, usually referred to as *Lecky's Wrinkles*. In 1872–4, as Lieutenant Lecky in command of the *Penguin* he was actively engaged in surveying these coasts, giving his name to a harbour, an inlet, a lookout, a monument, a retreat, and a shelf. To compile a history of the exploration and survey of the channels, with full biographical notes on the seamen of various nations who have lent their names to the all too numerous features, would be an absorbing task. A task only suitable, perhaps, for a man with a long vista of years ahead of him, one who was a linguist, and one who believed that labour is its own reward.

The weather still being foul we delayed starting until the following afternoon. While waiting a party went out in the dinghy and after a stern chase shot a steamer duck. Outside in the channel we found a fair wind. Setting all plain sail, and with the engine running, we did not have to touch the sheets until we had cleared Tarleton Pass at the opening of Nelson Strait. Although this strait opens directly on to the Pacific no swell reaches the eastern end owing to the number of islands. In the narrow channel between Vancouver and Evans Islands we again encountered head winds and had to beat up to Mayne harbour on the coast of Evans Island. In six hours sailing we had made good twenty-five miles much better than our average run which since leaving Punta Arenas had been only eighteen miles a day.

Before the channels were lit, when all vessels had to anchor at night, Mayne harbour was in constant use. On the plan of the harbour the narrow entrance is marked with buoys, but the buoys are no longer there. Next day, in a flat calm, we motored the remaining twenty miles to Puerto Bueno.

CHAPTER IX

PEEL INLET

The ice was here, the ice was there,
The ice was all around:
It cracked and growled, and roared and howled,
Like noises in a swound.

THE ANCIENT MARINER

A PLACE THAT HAS LONG FIGURED as the penultimate goal, the advance base or springboard into the unknown, is often given in one's mind unwarranted attributes. I can think of places in the Himalaya which from the map appear to be important road junctions or a natural jumping-off place for the crossing of some high pass; a place on which for many days the thoughts of the party have fondly dwelt— the sheep, eggs, butter, beer, or transport likely to be available—only to find on arrival a smoky hovel tenanted, if at all, by some ascetic bent on a solitary fast, who has chosen it as a spot where he will not be tempted to break it.

So, on the voyage out, had Puerto Bueno loomed large in our thoughts, but by now we had experience of the channels and had learnt to expect nothing anywhere, irrespective of whether a place was called a cove, a harbour, or a port. Only in this way were we not disappointed. In the old days, no doubt, a visitor to Puerto Bueno would at least have had company. It was a regular stopping place where, by begging or barter, one could probably make good any deficiencies. But ships do not go there now. There is a good, safe anchorage, where wood and water can be had for the labour, and that is all. It is supposed to have been discovered and named by Sarmiento who had been dispatched south from Peru to intercept Drake then thought to be on his way back through the Magellan Straits. But Drake went on westwards round the world and Sarmiento, after a thorough examination of the Straits, went on to Spain. Certainly the amount of wood which has been cut in the vicinity by ships' parties points to its having been a favourite harbour for a long time. Apart from this clearing, and an oil drum planted on a rock either as an ornament, a letter-box, or a leading mark, the place must be the same now as it was nearly four hundred years ago. In such surroundings it was easy to picture a three-masted carrack, not much more than twice *Mischief*'s size, with high carved poop and yellow painted sides, lying at anchor, while a boat-load of fierce, swarthy sailors rowed ashore.

In the belief that there would not be any safe harbour in Peel Inlet I had intended that *Mischief* should await the return of the shore party at Puerto Bueno. Now that we had seen the place the idea was less attractive. There seemed to be no life and little of interest in the neighbourhood to keep a party amused for two months. They could not even see passing ships, for the main channel is out of sight from the inner harbour. I was not surprised then when we left, to find that those who were to keep the ship were not looking forward to their stay at Puerto Bueno.

We left next morning, having first made sure that the navy had not already been here. The calm weather of the previous day contin-ued. There was no wind, no rain, no sun. Peel Inlet opens off Canal Sarmiento about eight miles north of Puerto Bueno round Cape Antonio. The northern side of the entrance is formed by the shore of Chatham Island and between cape and island, across the six-mile-wide entrance, are a few small islets. Off the shore of one of these a large object in the water arrested our attention, and when we realised it was not a boat but an ice floe we examined it with increased interest but with no great concern. A few miles up we passed the very narrow entrance to Pitt channel, a short cut leading to Canal San Andres and thence to the main channel. Several more floes, some of fantastic shape and delicate blue colouring, now drifted by close to the ship and were greeted with pleased cries, much as some ignorant clown might greet the first few ranging shots of a hostile battery. It is ridiculous to think that we went out of our way to photograph these feeble harbingers of the coming hordes.

When ahead of us a long line of what appeared to be white water was seen stretching almost from shore to shore, we at length awoke to the fact that trouble might be at hand. The mood of care-free happiness,

'In the fjords the prevailing gloom is lightened by magnificent streams of ice.' The cable is ranged on deck and both anchors, the 'fisherman' and the 'C.Q.R.' ready for letting go, but the staysail halyard seems to be coiled like grandmother's knitting

encouraged by the near accomplishment of the long outward passage and the closeness of our objective, changed rapidly to one of extreme anxiety, and made me wonder where we could go should Peel Inlet be blocked. These weak fears, engendered possibly by a diet of mussels, proved groundless. That which from afar had looked like almost solid ice, dissolved on approach to a mass of small floes (technically known as 'bergy bits') through which we had no difficulty in steering, though at a very slow pace. There were frequent leads of more open water and with a lookout posted in the bows to signal to the helmsman it was possible to avoid any serious collisions. If one appeared to be unavoidable a man with the boathook and another standing on the bobstay did what they could to deflect the floe. We were surprised, even alarmed, at the weight of impact of a floe no bigger than a small table. From the cross-trees it was possible to see well ahead and to plan one's course according to the shifting ice.

This accumulation of ice was encountered some fifteen miles up the inlet where it divides, a short arm running south-east and a much longer arm stretching north. The glacier which I had chosen from the map lies at the head of the south-east arm which is about four miles long. This comparatively short arm had another attraction for not far from the glacier at its head there is a cove called Caleta Amelia where the *Meteoro* (a 650-ton twin-screw steamer) with Skottsberg's party on board had spent two nights while Skottsberg and a geologist examined the shore at the foot of the glacier. As we opened up the south-east arm the glacier came in sight, a huge sheet of ice nearly two miles broad, cleft in its middle by a bald rocky hill, with its upper reaches shrouded in mist. It must have made a thrilling sight to those of the party to whom glaciers were unfamiliar. Even Charles and I were profoundly impressed by its size and by the way in which it flowed out into the deep waters of the fjord, suggesting to an observer the idea of inexhaustible, overflowing abundance, an unmistakable hint of the vastness of the snowfield from which it came. From the practical point of view we were pleased to note the easy angle of its descent, the relative smoothness of its tongue, and the presence of a convenient shelf of rock on which we could land.

We were still a long way off and in between lay a great deal of loose ice as well as half a mile or more of the chaotic water-borne part of the glacier itself, and as we closed the western shore to creep along to Caleta Amelia the thickening ice threatened to make even that unattainable. After poking about looking for a lead we gave it up. We could see where Amelia cove lay but as there was no getting there we had to anchor in another small cove a mile short of it. Three of us then embarked in the dinghy to see how near we could get to the glacier. By our later standards the ice cannot have been thick for we rowed for nearly an hour without having to pole away floes or to haul the dinghy between them with an ice-axe. But soon bigger floes barred our way and we drew alongside one on which we could land to survey the prospect. It was not encouraging. We were still a mile away from solid ice and owing to the dense forest on both shores it seemed as impossible to reach the glacier by land. In 1933 Michael Mason came here in a steam launch and from a photograph in his book *Where Tempests Blow* it seems that at that time the glacier was not split in two by the rock hill but flowed round it and united again at its foot thrusting out into the sea an unbroken front of twice the present width. Now only the ice stream to the north of the rock hill enters the water; the southern ice stream stops short a hundred yards from the shore. All along the seaward face of the rock hill, many feet above its present level, a distinct line of polished rock shows the height to which the ice once reached.

This setback was severe but was not necessarily fatal to our plans. Since the glacier on which we had set our hopes proved unattainable we had to find another. It seemed reasonable to think that of the many which flowed into the northern arm of Peel Inlet there would surely be one on which we could land. The amount of floating ice and the unexpected difficulty in landing had subdued us a little. All sorrows, we are told, are alleviated by eating bread. By this, no doubt, is meant food in general, but whether steamer duck should be called food is 'a point verging perilously on the moot'. Our duck had been hung for three days, boiled twice, cooked in a pressure cooker, and served curried, yet still it had about it a pungent flavour of steamer duck—that is, of fish oil. Many years have passed since the Rev. Dr Folliot justly observed that 'the science of fish sauce is by no means brought to perfection—a fine field of discovery still lies open in that line'; yet in Patagonia the field has been neglected, as yet no sauce has been discovered that will disguise the fishiness of steamer duck.

A 'wooding' party ashore at the second anchorage in Peel Inlet

Procter fending off small floes

To sail through these ice-strewn waters in a small boat not built with a view to shunting ice, where a boat needs to be able to twist and turn quickly, would be difficult and dangerous. Without an engine our difficulties would have been insurmountable. On motoring out next morning we steered for the eastern shore where the ice was less thick. Opposite the point where we had turned south-east on the previous day, a small cape projects, and 300 or 400 yards off this cape were several large floes. I was steering, and elected to pass between two of the biggest which were some fifty yards apart. Although we were watching them pretty intently, for they seemed to be unusually still, it was not until we were up to them that I realised they were aground. A moment later we joined them. There was no kelp to warn us and we were a long way off shore. Of course there was no need to have gone between the floes and any fool should have guessed that they were hard and fast from their appearance, for they were sticking high out of the water. We lowered the dinghy, ran out a kedge anchor, and pulled her off with less trouble than such carelessness deserved.

The northern arm which we were now entering is narrow and enclosed by high walls on both sides. Its western wall is formed by the large Wilcock peninsula with mountains running up to 5000 ft., and many small glaciers, none of which reaches the sea; while, of course, the eastern shore forms the foothills of the Cordillera 8000 or 9000 ft. above. It must be remembered that the latitude here is about that of London, and presumably it is the combined effects of the extent and height of this range together with the weather which accounts for the accumulation of snow and the consequent size of the glaciers. The permanent snow line in this latitude is about 3000 ft. It is said that the coolness of the summers rather than the severity of the winters is the most important factor in maintaining so low a snow line, the glaciers, and the snow field from which they descend. If we include the Darwin range in Tierra del Fuego (where the snow line is about 2000 ft.) this ice mantle covers a length of over 700 miles and is broken only at the Straits of Magellan and the Rio Baker, which separates the two great fields of inland ice at latitude 48°. The two together form the largest glaciated region of the temperate zone. Its northernmost glacier, the San Rafael, reaches the sea in lat. 46°40' S., further from the pole than any Alaskan glacier by ten degrees, and twenty degrees further than the Jokelfjord, the most southern of the Norwegian glaciers which reach the sea. Darwin puts it even more strikingly. He says of this San Rafael glacier, fifteen miles long and in one place seven miles broad, that it pushes its ice into the sea at a point on the coast where, within less than 500 miles, palms grow.

After some six miles of threading our way through patches of ice and occasional stretches of clear water we at last turned into a small bay to reconnoitre the approach to the next 'sea-level' glacier. Waterfall Bay, as we called it, was magnificent if nothing else. Quite near and high on our left a great white stream of ice swept round the foot of a black ridge to break into myriads of cracks, seracs, and crevasses, many of them scintillating with a vivid blue, as they plunged steeply to the ice-strewn water. On one side was bare rock; on the other, almost as steep, evergreen forest. On the other side of the bay, the waterfall itself which in any other bay would have been impressive, faded into insignificance before its stupendous, frozen counterpart. Here we could approach near to the glacier but we could see no likely landing place; and even suppose we did land, an ascent of the ice-fall was obviously impractical, while the rock on the left looked steep. The thought of having to make our first carry on untried legs up such steep rock daunted me. Charles was in two minds about it, but the longer I looked the more certain I became that it might do—but only as a last resort. Perhaps it was, that, as the time for abandoning the snug shelter of the ship drew inevitably nearer, the more ready I was to postpone it. Anyway it seemed wiser to enlarge the circle of our acquaintance before we finally committed ourselves, so, without dropping anchor we left the bay.

Several miles further north the fjord opens out into a wide reach, the eastern shore receding to form the entrance to what is called on the map Calvo inlet. Inside the inlet we could see three glaciers. There were several more in a very narrow extension of Calvo which penetrated inland for several miles, and yet another which terminated a mile from the sea on the north side of the entrance. Here were infinite riches in a little space. As the wide reach was free of ice we made sail and stood over to an island in the middle of the entrance hoping to find an anchorage. Here the water was deep, so we carried on and closed the northern shore where there was ice. Soon we were creeping through a narrow lead, with the shore close on our port hand and thick ice on the other. We began sounding, determined to anchor as soon as we found a reasonable depth, for evening was drawing on. At last we got eleven fathoms and let go the anchor; we were fifty yards from the shore and about a mile from the nearest glacier. On the whole the day had been fine with a few wintry gleams of sunshine. Thirty miles inland from the main channel in the lee of the imposing range on Wilcock peninsula, the absence of violent winds was most noticeable. Indeed the comparatively fair weather we enjoyed throughout our long stay in Calvo could only be attributed to the shielding effect of this high land.

Our plan now was to take *Mischief* as near as possible to the glacier immediately ahead of us. After a peaceful night in the ice we motored very slowly for an hour and a half through thick floes before we anchored again close in to the bank in six fathoms. As our cable rattled out steamer ducks scuttled away, a penguin bobbed up, and from a nearby cave a sea lion roared in astonishment. After lunch the shore party went off in the dinghy to reconnoitre. The floes were too close together for rowing so we either paddled or hauled ourselves along with the help of an ice-axe with which the bowman reached out, striking the point into the floe ahead. Having passed close under the cave where the sea lion lived with his harem we found an easy landing place, but upon climbing a rock ridge we discovered that an arm of the fjord lay between us and our objective. At the head of this little arm was another branch of the same glacier, but the little arm was chock-a-block with ice and the way along the shore looked long and difficult. But on the other side, where the main glacier ended abruptly in a hundred foot high ice-wall, a little sandy beach beckoned us invitingly. The beach was within fifty yards of the left bank of the glacier, and dare we but force *Mischief* through the ice to anchor there, one problem at least—that of ferrying our stores ashore—would be solved. Whether a way up the glacier could be found was another thing. That part of it overlooking the sea was impassable, but we had already noticed what looked like a small moraine on the flank of the glacier nearest to the beach. It appeared that the beach with its sand and boulders was in fact the termination of the moraine.

Because of the tide and wind the ice conditions in the bay were seldom static. Our first sight of the cove off the sandy beach showed it to be free of ice and the water between reasonably open. After tea, when we began moving, more ice, including some very large floes, had drifted in. This was added to by the continual discharge of ice from the glacier snout, from which, with a thunderous roar, hundred of tons of ice crashed frequently into the water, setting up a young tidal wave. Hardening our hearts we drove the long-suffering *Mischief* slowly through a mile of thickly clustering floes, mindful only of her propeller. The shape of a floe above water is no indication of what goes on below and there was always the danger of a floe capsizing under our counter on to the propeller as we brushed past. At last this frightening and heartrending shunting of ice came to an end and by 8 o'clock we had *Mischief* anchored in seven fathoms only fifty yards from the beach.

As anchorages go this one was more spectacular than safe. Within a stone's throw of us there was on the one hand a fantastically furrowed cliff of sapphire blue ice; on the other, and equally close, a heavily forested cliff; while around us lay a slowly circling mass of floes of alarming size, some of them as big as a cottage with the garden thrown in. Although we had reached the haven of our choice I was far from tranquil. It was obvious that more reconnoitring must be done before the shore party could disembark. It was more than possible that if more ice drifted in the ship might not be able to leave or might even be pushed on to the beach. Already the knocking about sustained by poor *Mischief* and her tender was reacting upon her owner as if he had suffered in person; indeed, what with chilblains, back-ache, and a stiff knee his sufferings were at that time not merely vicarious. Even Charles, as our short excursion of the morning showed, was not as spry as he might have been, for he moved with more dignity and deliberation than the occasion demanded.

Next day, Friday, 16 December, we went ashore to try our luck on the moraine. Compared with Himalayan moraines it was despicably small and failed miserably in offering the easy going that they generally provide. (The absence of well developed moraines was a characteristic of all the glaciers we saw.) About half a mile up from the shore, toiling mainly in the trough between ice and moraine or moraine and jungle, we met the first obstacle, a twenty feet high wet slab up which obviously the loads would have to be hauled. About a like distance beyond this we met the type of obstacle we had half expected—a place

The south-east end of Peel Inlet with the glacier we had hoped to land on in the background; the line of ice-worn rock, showing where the glacier at one time reached, is clearly seen

The snout of the Calvo glacier from the ship

where the ice so impinged against a rock wall that it left us no way through, round, or over. Thus we were forced to seek a way on the glacier itself which at this point proved more accommodating. We found it to be made up of a series of transverse crevasses, the ridges between them being sometimes very narrow and sometimes a yard or two wide. Where two crevasses merged together, as they often did, there was a void, and where two ridges met there was a pinnacle. On the whole it was a labyrinth which Charles tackled with more optimism than I felt justified, but after about an hour's hard work, finding a way mainly by trial and error, we emerged in mid-glacier on more or less unbroken ice. So far so good. Heading up the glacier in a crevasse-free trough we gained another 500 ft. of height before becoming entangled in a frightful jumble of seracs and yawning chasms. Above and beyond this devastated region we saw what appeared to be a flat shelf promising better going, but there was no reaching it that day.

The weather had been kind. True, it drizzled incessantly but it had been quite calm. When we got back to the shore at 6 o'clock we found that more ice had drifted in. Between ship and shore it lay so thickly that we had to haul ourselves back to the ship by means of a rope. We learnt that down here there had been a lot of wind which had brought into the cove some gigantic bergs. The ship's party had had an anxious time, watching helplessly as these monsters closed in scraping the ship's side and threatening to crush her, for the ice to seaward was by then too thick to permit escape. The pressure of the ice lifted the dinghy out of the water till it perched forlornly on a big floe. All they could do was to try to stop the bigger bergs from touching the rudder or fouling the bobstay, the bowsprit shrouds, or the bowsprit itself. As soon as the wind dropped, which it did as suddenly as it had begun, the ice began to drift out so that when we returned we saw only the aftermath of this heavy onslaught.

On the whole, despite the inconclusive nature of our reconnaissance, it seemed best for us to gamble on finding a route to the ice-cap by way of what we now called the Calvo glacier; for there are few ice-falls which time and perseverance will not overcome. The essential thing was to get the ship away as early as possible. The morning's inrush of ice had forced her perceptibly nearer the shore and the night's happenings emphasised strongly that this was no place to linger. About midnight an appalling crash close alongside brought us all on deck with a run. We were in time to see the water still boiling and surging and blocks of ice shooting up from below. One of our bigger neighbours had capsized and had broken up with all the turmoil and upheaval of water that would accompany the death throes of a stricken whale.

In the morning, except for two monsters which lay menacingly close, the cove was free of ice. Having made our decision we set about sorting stores and getting them ashore while the water remained open. In the cabin Chaos and old Night reigned. John and I checked food against food lists and filled paraffin containers, while the others weeded out their climbing kit from among sea clothes. Charles' impedimenta for journeying by land and sea for the first time lay remorselessly revealed. From time to time brief glimpses of his treasures had aroused our curiosity and now Michael was able to complete the inventory he had thought it worth while surreptitiously making, either in furtherance of his sociological studies or with a view to equipping himself for some future journey on the lines of his illustrious model. A copy of this inventory which he kindly gave me, perhaps merits insertion here rather than in the obscurity of an appendix:

One tin of anchovies and two of sardines.

Palm and sail needle.

An old piece of canvas.

Yachting cap.

Tattered Balaclava helmet (looks like a crown of thorns).

Assorted empty tins of all shapes and sizes, mostly rusty.

Old pieces of string and cloth.

Assorted buttons.

Salt and pepper in empty first-aid tins.

A pair of pliers.

Rusty knife on an enormous khaki lanyard.

Old sweater and wind jacket, torn to shreds.

Patches with bits of trouser attached, once grey flannels.

A pack of cards, incomplete.

A sextant, too venerable to be cleaned.

Some maps and charts of S. America in general.

Selection of *Reader's Digests*.

A tin of pea-nuts.

Ancient camera, operated by guess work.

Bottle of quinine.

Home-made solid fuel burner with bits of 'Meta'.

Dipping pen and ink bottle with huge cork in silver container.
Compass and binoculars.
Thick tailor's tape measure.
Assorted spices in small tins.
Dilapidated billy-can, half rusted through.

A pair of mittens of very original design.
Badminton Library *Yachting*—very heavy.
Some whisky.
Hooded climbing jacket, homemade.

Although the glass was rising rain fell all day. We ferried the stores ashore, pitched the two tents, and left the stores inside. In the afternoon we made another reconnaissance but it did nothing towards clearing away our doubts. On the next day, with the willing help of the ship's party in carrying loads, we hoped we should be able to make a flying start.

CHAPTER X

THE CALVO GLACIER

Still and blanched and cold and lone,
The icy hills far from me
With frosty ulys overgrown
Stand in their sculptured secrecy.

DE LA MARE

It is a curious fact that although knowing full well that one will soon be wet through, one always shrinks from starting out wet. After a wet night, rain was still falling and, far from being in a state of raring to go, the shore party sat in the cabin that morning looking like men meditating a cold plunge or even suicide. By 10 o'clock, when there was merely drizzle, and the crew in their oilskins were wondering why we still dithered, any more convincing excuses for delay were hard to find. With the air of dedicated men we began to pack our rucksacks, the last loads to go ashore. Having finished, I in my turn became impatient, and stood, pawing the deck, so to speak, holding the dinghy painter in one hand and an ice-axe in the other; while Jorge, always a slow packer, persistently called out in Spanish enquiring if such or such a thing were necessary; to which, I, neither understanding what he said nor able to see through the deck, invariably and confidently answered 'No', which is Spanish, I believe for 'No'.

Having landed we then had to make up five loads for the first carry, leaving John behind to mind the ship. The large number of tins of 'Lifeboat' biscuits to be carried—flour is no use with Primus stove cooking—gave us some troublesome loads, but we had with us three Yukon pack-boards on which with patience and a little ingenuity one can securely fasten the queerest loads. Jorge, as befitted his youth, shouldered the biggest load, with Mike not far behind. Having hoisted these to the top of the slab, where we had already put a fixed rope, and dumped them there, we all returned to the shore to say goodbye, for

I was anxious for the ship to leave. The instructions I had given were that they must return to Puerto Bueno and remain there until 1 January, by which time the navy might have delivered the petrol and paraffin. Then they were to come back, cruise in the bay a few miles off the glacier, and look out for any signs of us. There was plenty of wood for us to make a fire and our bright yellow tents would be readily spotted. This manoeuvre was to be repeated every Sunday until 12 February, the ship meantime lying at a safe anchorage in Calvo fjord —if they found one—or back at Puerto Bueno. The shore party had fifty days' food so that we could survive until the middle of February; in fact, I intended, if it was at all possible, to make our ice-cap crossing and return here by the end of January; if we had not shown up by 12 February they were to allow us one week's grace before making their way back to Punta Arenas. The early return on 1 January and the subsequent weekly sighting of our base-camp seemed advisable. It was always possible that if we met with some mischance or had failed in our project that we might wish to be picked up at an early date. It was not an ideal arrangement but in the circumstances I could think of nothing better. I did not want *Mischief* to move about more than was necessary and at the same time I wanted to be sure that the shore party would not have to wait weeks on the beach should they return unexpectedly soon.

In the afternoon the weather cleared up. We carried more loads to the beginning of the ice route, and on the steep moraine between ice and forest we carved out two tent platforms for Camp II. As we trudged back down the moraine with the blue waters of the bay spread out below us, the setting sun shone on the myriad ice floes and upon our small ship beyond. As our tents were pitched we had nothing more to do but collect firewood and start a fire. Considering that rain is an almost daily occurrence it was surprising how easily this was done. Perhaps we inadvertently hit on the 'tepu' tree, for even when we left the channels for good we were still a little hazy about the precise identity of this tree. Charles and Jorge shared a high-altitude Meade tent with sleeve entrance, while I had a one-man tent, so shaped that it resembled nothing so much as a coffin with its lid propped up invitingly. Although sharing a tent these two probably had more elbow room than I who shared mine with the Primus stove, the 'ready-use' stores, saucepans of water or snow, and such like. As

I knew what food and paraffin we had and was responsible for them lasting, it was only right that I should attend to the rations and such cooking as there was.

With nothing whatever in the way of food to look for beyond what we could carry and having to carry enough for seven weeks, every ounce had to be of value. In other words the kinds of food we needed had to be chosen on the lines of an Antarctic sledging ration, in which calories are solemnly calculated, rather than a Himalayan ration; for in high climbing the cry is usually 'give us the luxuries and we will dispense with the necessities'. Besides such basic belly-timber as pemmican, biscuit, sugar, and butter (at the rate of eight, seven, six and three ounces, respectively per man-day) we did have some luxuries such as tea, cheese, chocolate, dried skim-milk, raisins, egg-powder, and oatmeal. The cheese, egg-powder and oatmeal were only for use on alternate days but in the event they did not work out even as well as that. The full allowance for each man was about twenty-nine ounces a day.

This diet must have been totally lacking in vitamins unless perhaps some lurked in the tinned butter. I cannot think that there are any more in pemmican than in a slab of gun-cotton, and since the biscuit was in sealed tins there was no chance of its becoming vitalised by weevils and maggots as was the case in the days of the old sailing ships. Six weeks—the time we were ashore—is no doubt too short a time for the ill effects of such a diet to make themselves felt; but in the three months between Punta Arenas and Valparaiso we did not eat any fresh vegetables other than some rather poor potatoes which were soon finished. Apparently one can do very well without vegetables. In some countries only the rich can afford them and in others they are the only food the poor have to live on. Beau Brummel, who no doubt could afford vegetables and who lived to what was in his day the ripe age of sixty-two, when asked if he never ate vegetables confessed that he 'once ate a pea'. The more a man travels in remote regions the more will he think how right Thoreau was 'that most of the luxuries and nearly all the so-called comforts of life are not only not indispensable but positive hindrances to the elevation of mankind'.

We devoted the next day to moving everything to Camp II about 700 ft higher up the moraine. This involved two journeys up and down and a third to carry forward what we had left at the half-way dump

Charles and Jorge prospecting a route through typical ice on the
lower Calvo glacier

by the slabs. At this early stage, before we had made any inroads on our loads by eating or by throwing away what had been misguidedly thought indispensable, the total weight to be moved was about 475lb.— that is to say three carries of over 50lb. a man. The food accounted for over 300lb., a figure which, of course, included much inedible packing material. In this respect the biscuit, packed as it was in at least twelve pounds of tin, was the worst offender. 'Satu', the toasted flour which is used in the Himalaya and which can be carried in a sack is, of course, the answer, and had I been a little more alert we could have had it. Not until we reached Valparaiso did we discover that the same thing ('harina tostada') is in common use and easily procurable. Later we took such a supply on board, and although the others did not take it in their tea— as one should—they all liked it.

The pemmican, a very palatable, full-bodied Danish brand, with a grip o' the gob such as Jorrocks liked in his favourite port, was merely wrapped in silver paper in one-pound slabs. Greaseproof paper, from which at a pinch the starving explorer might extract some nourishment, would have been lighter and better. Nowadays, such is the march of science, some weight can be saved by using polythene containers for paraffin instead of clumsy tins. Although it was at the expense of the ship's party we had not stinted ourselves of paraffin, for when living on a glacier paraffin is not a thing one wants to be short of. We had about thirty pounds of it to carry and it proved to be too much, for the quantity used depends on whether water is available or snow has to be melted. Having found by trial how many meals a full stove could cook, we dumped a gallon on the glacier intending to retrieve it on our return. Our three personal loads must have weighed nearly 100 lb. altogether. Jorge had too much, my load erred on the same side, while Charles had too little. Either because of inexperience or excessive zeal for travelling light he had not brought anything to put under his sleeping bag. This was such a serious omission that we cut up our big ground sheet and gave him half.

After tea we improved the first part of the ice route by cutting steps, for while one can balance along so-called knife-edge ridges, make giant strides, or jump when unencumbered, one's movements are much more restricted when shouldering a heavy load. A mountaineer normally moves with care, but cut off as we were from any outside help we needed to be doubly careful. On one occasion, as will appear, I did not exercise care enough. After a night of heavy rain I was discouraged to find pools of water at the foot of my 'coffin'. I removed this nuisance by stabbing holes in the floor at strategic points thereby making a sort of self-draining cockpit like *Mischief*'s.

Feeling that we might have overlooked some loophole at the point where the glacier met the rock wall, we examined it more thoroughly but with no more success. The search led us through a narrow tunnel between dripping ice and dripping rock until the rock wall receded. Here, on a bed of gravel, we found growing in close profusion a bank of bright scarlet trumpet-shaped flowers with large dark green leaves— a sight the more beautiful and cheering in the dank gloom of their surroundings. These were later identified as *Ourisia alpina*. After lunching in mid-glacier we ascended as far as the 'devastated area' where we zigzagged about until brought up short by a chasm that could not be turned. Unable to go further up the glacier we began to make for its far side. By a long, intricate, and slightly dangerous route we eventually arrived. To our relief this bank (the true right side) of the glacier consisted of unbroken ice and it seemed likely that the flank of the 'devastated area' could thereby be turned and the shelf gained. This was something, but we returned to camp only a little less dejected for none of us thought the route feasible for a laden party. I took comfort from my companions. Jorge proved active, nimble, and safe, having perfect balance; while Charles, though a little slow, had a wonderful memory for a route, an invaluable faculty in an ice maze where it is so easy to lose the line and hard to recover it— especially when a party has been moving fast and has cut only a minimum of steps.

Even after having a pint of pemmican which should have produced in me more robust thoughts, I was still haunted by a fear that the Calvo glacier might be too much for us. The alternative line, involving a climb of nearly 2000 ft. through the forest above the moraine, had been unanimously rejected. This forest clung to precipitous slopes, slabby in parts and seamed with gullies, and was such a matted tangle of living and rotten, fallen trees, that the carrying of loads up that distance was out of the question. Out of curiosity on one occasion I had penetrated a few yards into it near Camp II where it was not even steep, and had recoiled in horror.

Looking across the lower Calvo which had to be crossed and recrossed; the glacier on the left with the well-marked medial moraine is a branch of the Calvo which divides from it two miles up above the rock 'island' in the foreground; Camp III was at the upper end of the island where the glacier divides

The morning broke wet. It was important, I felt, to maintain the impetus of the attack, so we made a carry to a dump on the glacier and then poked about half-heartedly in the rain looking for a better route to the right bank. Making no progress on my chosen line I stood surveying the troubled sea of ice looking for a smooth patch. Deceived by what from that distance looked like a promising lead through the 'devastated area' to the shelf above, Jorge and I set off hot-foot. By an incredibly bad route which promised to become worse, we did get nearly to the shelf. The higher we climbed the wider and deeper became the chasms and the more profuse and haphazardly heaped the great blocks of ice which half filled them. Nor were these blocks resting on solid bottom. Jorge, while balancing on one and gazing downwards, withdrew hastily, reporting, 'No bottle'. As well as the perils below there were perils from above, and one had to keep an eye lifting to the towering and tottering seracs from which this debris came. We returned to camp very wet. Things were not looking at all rosy; it seemed that we could hardly have selected a worse glacier for our experiment. Had Jorge asked my opinion and had I known Spanish I could only have told him that our situation was hopeless but not desperate.

Our fifth day ashore was another sunless day of showers. Since landing we had scarcely seen the sun, but at least there had been no wind to bother us. Although our hope of ultimately finding a route was not good we carried more loads to the dump in mid-glacier before continuing the search. When we reached the half-mile wide belt of crevasses and seracs between us and the far side we separated in order to probe it in several places. It was not sound mountaineering practice but it was the quickest way of 'exploring every avenue'. My chosen line promised so well that having got halfway I whistled up Charles who had retired from his, momentarily baffled. With mounting excitement, expecting every moment to be stopped by some impassable gap, we pressed on towards the promised land—for so we had come to regard our very modest objective, the opposite side of the glacier. Once we could see the smooth ice beyond we were not long in reaching it. At last facing up the glacier instead of across it, we moved rapidly over comparatively unbroken ice until we reached the outer edge of the devastated area. Here it was neither so wide nor so broken and very soon we had gained the shelf. So far as we could see this ran diagonally right across to the left bank (on which Camp II lay) and it would bring us out well above the rock wall where with any luck there would be more moraine. Meanwhile there was a pleasant site for Camp III on a rock promontory on the right bank.

On returning to Camp II at seven that evening my eyes were smarting. In such dull weather on dry glacier it had seemed unnecessary to wear snow glasses, but evidently the greater height had increased the glare enough to cause snow blindness. By morning the pain was acute. As the day happened to be fine, with a watery sun struggling to pierce the cloud, we took a rest and spread our wet sleeping bags to dry.

On the 24th we spent five and a half hours in moving to Camp III, the height by barometer being 1500 ft. Though not at all easy to find, the route went well and we did what we could to mark and improve it by cutting large steps; for except in the middle trough there was a complete absence of stones to build cairns. As is often the way after an off-day the party moved with less vigour than before and I had time to cut a staircase off the ice and to level a tent site before the other two arrived. Even with rain falling it was an admirable spot. The rocky promontory formed a sort of island which rose to about 500 ft. above the glacier. Round it wound the two arms of the Calvo glacier; one we had just crossed; the other, flowing round its north side, was the one whose tongue we had seen at the head of the little fjord on our first reconnaissance. There was firewood at hand and just below our tents were several little tarns. We felt better in every way. We were in a better camp site and a better frame of mind. Had it not been for the accursed rain, a pressing shortage of tobacco, and for the fact that we were so wet, I could have burst into song. It was Christmas Eve and appropriately enough I had ten socks hanging from my tent roof to dry.

Christmas Day dawned gloriously fine. A six-hour journey down to the dump in the middle of the glacier left us feeling disinclined for more. We brewed up twice—a very exceptional indulgence—and although it was midsummer gathered our winter fuel. While we were so employed a pair of duck settled on the tarn below; their bronze breasts, dove grey necks, and white wings showed that they were of the same species as those John had shot at Columbine cove. Climbing to the top of the 500 ft. hill behind our camp we looked down upon the

Looking back to the fjord from the shelf above the 'devastated area';
the mountains of the Wilcock peninsula in the background

Looking north across the glacier from Camp V (c. 4000 ft.)

undivided Calvo glacier, a width of some two miles. Our shelf running across the glacier appeared to break into chaos and ruin well short of the dry land of the left bank. Far in the distance, beyond a daunting sea of pinnacles, smooth unbroken *névé* led without interruption to the skyline ridge. Pondering on these observations we returned to our Christmas pemmican with mixed feelings.

Boxing Day might well have seen the end of our immediate hopes. Not because of any major tragedy but because we had lost a pair of snow glasses. Having gone down to fetch the remaining loads we were moving independently and unroped up the unbroken part of the glacier not far from camp. Hereabouts were several open crevasses which could be either turned or crossed with a long stride. My load was unwieldy; a two gallon tin of paraffin had been tied to the top. It was so badly balanced that when I reached out to make a long stride over a crevasse the load swung round and dragged me down. Though fully wide enough at the surface to engulf a man and his load, further down this crevasse narrowed, so that at about fifteen feet below I became firmly wedged, unable to move hand, foot, or even my head. What might have easily made matters worse was the fact that I was stupidly carrying both ropes, the one we had recently been using and our spare. Jorge, recovering quickly from his dismay at seeing me thus swallowed up, was soon on the spot and began cutting steps down. Having released my load and passed the rope to Charles, they pulled that up, and eventually I was pulled out, too, like a cork out of a bottle. I still had my axe, but the snow glasses which had been pushed up on my forehead were far down in the Calvo. Had Jorge not had a spare pair (one of the things, possibly, he had not consulted me about when packing) we might have been Rubiconed. In the Karakoram the hardy, rough-hewn men of Askole when crossing snowfields either wear home-made goggles, cardboard with a narrow slit, or merely daub soot around their eyes. But they do not do this for more than a day's march and even then their consequent sufferings seem to be almost as great as if they had worn nothing. Apart from a scratched face and a slightly wrenched shoulder no damage had been done. All the loads being at Camp III we now could start unravelling the next knot in this intricate tangle. For this Calvo glacier presented a problem only a little less interesting than the finding of a route up a mountain. Owing to the rise of the glacier we could not see more than a mile ahead and as yet we had no hint of where the *névé* began. We thought probably a thousand feet higher. Although above the promontory the undivided glacier is as wide again as the branch we had crossed, in this wider field of possibilities only the shelf leading towards the left bank seemed to offer any chance. Except for this smooth shelf, the huge sweep of ice resembled a piece of corrugated iron. Had the ridges been intact they might have offered a highway in either direction, but they were broken in so many places by longitudinal crevasses that the nett result was a series of disconnected ice islands. No doubt in the course of movement and melting these islands ultimately formed the seracs and craters of the lower reaches of the glacier. Anyhow no upward progress on the glacier itself could yet be made. We had to escape to the left bank and trust to reaching the *névé* that way.

As we had feared the smooth shelf ended a good quarter mile short of the left bank. Between shelf and bank lay the roughest sea of ice we had yet to cross. By a precarious route, involving the crossing of several frail snow bridges, we reached the ablation valley lying between glacier and rock well above the rock wall. Could we only find a better approach the ablation valley would lead us gently eastwards and upwards. A lower route was worse; we even explored a traverse which took us back above the rock wall through the forest. This fortunately would not go, for it would have meant our starting again from Camp II.

As nothing else offered we returned to it next day, carrying loads to a halfway dump, and set about improving the route. After much trial and error, having made the route much longer but less hazardous, we reached the trough again and went up it, crossing a number of avalanche cones which had fallen from the slopes above. These slopes, sparsely covered with grass, were too steep for a camp site and we had to make do with one on the moraine half a mile up where there was a stream. From a rock bluff 500 ft. higher we gazed upon a most satisfying scene. A little way ahead the trough opened out into a shallow snow-filled valley, merging on one side into the *névé*-covered glacier and on the other into the snow slopes of the mountain which flanked it. Several miles away the glacier disappeared from view as it swept round a high rock buttress thrown out by a ridge of the same mountain.

Across the glacier on the far side was a magnificent wall of rock and ice which dipped gradually to the place where we thought our col must lie, and the white carpet spread so glisteningly between these mountain walls would assuredly lead us there. Though the carpet might be horribly soft and deeply crevassed we had but to follow where it led.

The soaking we got from a hailstorm on the way back hardly damped the satisfaction we now felt. Provided the pass would go there was now nothing to stop us. We were not yet drunk with hope but Charles was elated enough by our brightening prospects to suggest a day off. Mindful of the effects of our last rest I compromised for a half day for him only, so while Jorge and I carried a load to the new camp site Charles left his at the halfway dump. The next day we moved camp and on the following day brought forward all that remained at the dump. It was 31 December. Thus a fortnight had been spent in establishing ourselves at 2600 ft. at a place where we were at last clear of the difficult part of the glacier and whence our further progress would be faster and straighter. By leaving a small food dump here for the return journey and by getting rid of some unwanted tins we could reduce our lifts from three to two. I had already made up my mind that the return journey would not be by way of the glacier. Melting was increasing fast and the snow bridges on the last section would by then be down. Another route would obviously have to be found. It seemed possible that by climbing from this Camp IV for about 2000 ft. over rock and snow until we were above Camp II we could then drop down to it. Though we could not climb up through the forest we could certainly force a way down.

CHAPTER XI

THE CALVO PASS

The vagrant merchant under a heavy load
Bent as he moves and needing frequent rest.

WORDSWORTH

THE FIRST OF JANUARY 1956, cloudless, windless, hot, was a better day even than Christmas Day. After plodding up the shallow snow-filled valley for about a mile we finally emerged at a col on the ridge dividing Calvo glacier from the valley to the south. Steep snow slopes dropped to a hanging valley containing a large lake while far below was a narrow ice-filled fjord with three big glaciers which crept down to its farther shore. This was the easterly extension of Calvo inlet which runs inland for another eight miles. It appeared so narrow and so choked with ice that we were glad we had ignored it.

We descended to our glacier by an easy snow slope, carefully picking our way through the maze of crevasses which were now just beginning to open. But the higher we went the less obvious did they become. Sometimes, only a barely perceptible crease in the unruffled surface betrayed a crevasse below. Sometimes there was no sign at all. We moved circumspectly at the full length of the rope, the leader prodding diligently the while. Sometimes a foot would go through and, then, after a brief but sufficing glimpse of frosty blue walls leading down to horrid depths, he would flounder over on his stomach or be hauled out on his back to the accompaniment of superfluous advice to use more care. Five hours of this in soft snow and sunshine was enough. At 3600 ft. by aneroid we dumped our loads and plodded homewards in the same steps. This precaution together with a cold night consolidated the trail. Next day we carried more loads to half a mile beyond the dump and then brought that forward as well. It was another gloriously sunny day. The snow softened and we soon got wet. The best part of the day was when we stepped from deep, wet snow on to warm, dry rocks,

Camp VI (c. 5000 ft.) and an unnamed peak on the north
containing wall of the glacier

feeling like tired swimmers wading ashore. These, however, were the
last rocks we should tread. This was the last water, too, that we should
find. In future we should have to melt snow. We therefore brewed tea
twice and laced our pemmican with chilli paste for the last time, for two
days of sun on snow had played havoc with our lips.

When rain set in early next morning we regretted not having
moved camp when it was fine. For it is most discouraging to pack up
in the rain and to strike wet tents knowing that they will be so much
the heavier to carry. Nevertheless, having reached the new camp we
went back to the dump for more loads before calling it a day. Snow
which fell throughout the night disclosed more faults in the design of
my tent. Without the protecting eave and a short vertical piece at the
side such as in a Meade, it allowed the accumulating snow to press the
sides inwards until the cursing inmate found it impossible to move or
turn without touching the fabric and starting copious leaks. This, however, was not the sum of my troubles. Charles, who was complaining
of sore feet, now expressed a doubt as to whether he would be able to
go on for many more days. But he decided to start and we set off with
light loads. Soon crevasses forced us on to the slopes on our right. We
traversed here for fully a mile before we could strike back to the middle
of the glacier. We stopped early because of Charles' feet and on the
way back I had plenty to think about. The success of the expedition
now seemed in jeopardy. The whole glacier was so crevassed and they
were so difficult to detect that it was unsafe to be on it with a party of
less than three. Should Charles decide to give up, we should have to
return. It was a decision that would have to be made overnight, for
only if we started back next day, a Thursday, could we be in time to
signal *Mischief* on her second appearance.

Next morning I was greatly relieved when Charles gamely decided
to go on, but had I realised the true state of affairs I might well have
hesitated before agreeing. He took a day off while Jorge and I did a
carry to the dump and then went on for an hour beyond it to select
a site for Camp VI. To talk of selecting camp sites in a uniform snow
desert sounds absurd. Indeed, they usually turned out to be those
places where the party sat down, as it were for the count, and failed to
get up. A little probing to make sure we were not over a crevasse and
there we were. Camp VI in such way had been chosen before we had

advanced far enough to see the end of the glacier, for we had not yet rounded the rock buttress. But the wall of rock and ice on the opposite side had almost ceased to dip, suggesting that there lay the lowest part of the ice-cap. It had been another fine, hot day. Such a day of overpowering brilliance that the dazzle and the heat striking up from the snow reduced us to the state of some early travellers in the Alps, in need only of an umbrella and a scent bottle.

Such brazenly fine days seemed unnatural after what we had expected. Next day, however, made amends with a terrible storm which began at four in the morning and continued until the afternoon. The wind battered at my tent as though bent on its destruction. The fabric, which was inadequately stayed, flapped wildly and incessantly, and when bursts of hail accompanied the gusts of wind the noise was frightening. Lying thus stormbound, pressing with hands or feet against the fabric in order to tauten and quieten it, I had leisure to reflect upon the folly of voluntarily taking rest days when in all certainty too many idle days would sooner or later be forced upon us by bad weather. On a journey such as this in which the time available for crossing the ice-cap and returning depended on the amount of food carried, an idle day means so much wasted food, and is something to be regarded with the gravest misgiving. On the other hand when the weather allows no choice in the matter idleness can be endured, perhaps even enjoyed, with no pricking of one's conscience. As Lord Curzon used to say: 'It is inevitable, therefore it can be approved'. Although the tents were close together the incessant din prevented my passing on to the others for their consideration the fruits of my profound reflections. Indeed, all talk between us was impossible. As by now I had no tobacco and my only book had been already read twice my resignation was sorely tried. I had already experimented with the smoking of our used tea leaves and had found that whether they were sun dried or toasted over the Primus the smoke was a little acrid. Now, carrying the experiment further, I found that fresh, unused tea smoked very well, and henceforth, regarding it as the quarter-master's perquisite, I allowed myself one pipeful a day.

A cold, clear night succeeded the storm and in the morning as we moved up to Camp VI we found the snow delightfully crisp. A stormy night was the prelude to another blizzard and another idle morning.

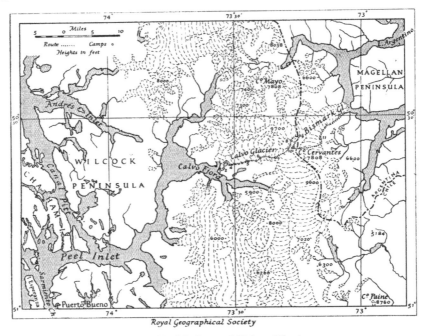

Royal Geographical Society

Map 2: Peel Inlet and Calvo Glacier
(Reproduced by permission of the Royal Geographical Society)

When the wind abated at 2 o'clock, thinking anything better than iner-
tia, I turned out the others. We climbed up unladen for two hours with
the idea of preparing the track for the next day. The wind, which was
at our backs, seemed to be rising again, and when we turned for home
we found ourselves facing half a gale and clouds of driven snow. The
landmarks disappeared one by one and soon it became questionable
whether or no our outgoing tracks would remain visible or be blot-
ted out before we sighted the tents. Very cold and wet we were, and
mightily relieved, when at length they loomed ahead. Charles' Spanish
and Jorge's English enabled them to converse deliberately, tortuously,
but not quite incomprehensibly, and as they lay in their sleeping bags,
restoring their half-frozen feet and discussing their pemmican, they no
doubt said things about this brief sortie which the noise of the storm
happily prevented my hearing.

When we started next morning in a brief lull the futility of the sortie of the evening before became even more apparent for not a vestige of a track remained. Half an hour later, when snow began to fall, we dumped the loads and fled. We tried once more in the afternoon only to be driven back when the mounting gloom of clouds rolling up the glacier threatened a repetition of yesterday's storm.

But for the time being the weather had done its worst. Our next carry took us beyond the rock buttress and brought into view the full width of the pass—a shallow flattening in the skyline ridge. On a day of stern plodding in bad snow and muggy weather, the leader's half-hour spell of stamping a track seemed never ending. If one glanced at one's watch, time stood still. I found the only way to keep going was to count one's steps.

In these regions a fine day is a thing to be remembered, not so much by its rareness—we were blessed with a good many— but for its perfection. Here are no grudging half measures. The sun blazes benignly from a cloudless sky upon mountains outlined starkly against a brilliant blue. Not a stone sullies the dazzling whiteness of the snow, the only rock in sight is the living rock of the mountains, for no stone ever seems to fall. On these lovely days there is not a breath of air to disturb the serenity of a frozen world suffused with light and warmth. Our spirits and strength restored by the invigorating influence of such a day we reached the dump and went on for another hour before making camp. The height of this Camp VII was 5750 ft. and we judged it to be about 500 ft. below the pass. After tea we brought the loads up from the dump, cooked supper and turned in, for it had become very cold.

We went to bed rather pleased with ourselves, the weather, and life in general; but within an hour a blizzard raged. Fearing that the incessant flapping would start a seam in the fabric of the tent I spent most of the night supporting the panels with alternate hands (for this exercise one had to wear gloves) until the snow banking up outside made the task unnecessary. Most of the snow had, I think, drifted, but quite obviously whether it had fallen or drifted it would not do for us to be caught away from camp in one of these sudden storms. By noon the storm had passed leaving in its wake a white mist which seemed to increase tenfold the heat of the unseen sun. In the afternoon we took some loads up to what appeared to be the highest part of the pass.

The rock buttress at the end of the rock ridge which runs north from Cervantes peak, with the main Bismarck glacier on the left and the East Bismarck glacier joining it from the right; we went down the ridge to the col short of the rocks and traversed the snow slope to the right to look down the the East Bismarck glacier. A bit of the lake can just be seen round a pinnacle about the centre of the rock buttress

Looking north from Camp IX (c. 7000 ft.); beyond the wide gap is the deep rift where an arm of the lake runs westwards to within five miles of the north-east end of Peel Inlet

Eastwards everything was hidden in a sea of mist, but to the south-west a deep notch between two mountains showed where yet another glacier rolled down to the eastern end of Calvo fjord.

The extremely violent changes of weather baffled prediction. Reputedly, the fairer the hostess the fouler the reckoning, and in the same way we suspected that the more brilliant the day the worse would be the next. The suspicion proved unfounded, for we now experienced two such successive days. They could not have been more timely. Friday, 13 January, was the first of these marvellous blue days. By 9 o'clock of a fresh, cool morning, filled with the exuberance which climbing swiftly on crisp snow affords, we had reached the dump. Having already resolved to do no more relaying we looked at the dump and what we had just added to it with some concern and our exuberance diminished. When we shouldered the newly made-up loads it disappeared for good. As we started contouring round the foot of the ridge on the north side of the pass the crisp snow began to give way under our feet.

We were now traversing a slightly undulating snow field, bounded on the east by a high ridge carrying a peak named on the map Cerro Cervantes (7,808 ft.). Although the snowfield fell away gradually towards a gap in the ridge which roused our interest and caused some discussion, we ignored it and shaped our course to a little north of east to where the great Bismarck glacier, which flows into Lake Argentino, originates. Still gaining height we plodded on slowly in increasing heat and softening snow. Wordsworth would have recognised us instantly as vagrant merchants, very bent and needing very frequent rest. By 3 o'clock we had drawn nearly level with the north end of the Cervantes ridge. Ahead of us lay a crest and, slight though it was, it effectually hid everything beyond. But we had had enough. So we camped and brewed tea before walking on to this insignificant crest.

The approach to an unknown pass to look over into unknown country is as exciting as the last pitch of a first ascent; and when the pass lies on a frontier and also forms the watershed between two oceans the thrill is intensified. Ideally, of course, the pass should be steep on both sides, so that one moment the climber sees nothing but the rock or snow in front of him and the next, as though a curtain had been drawn aside, a vast and unexpected landscape. But one can't have everything. Our crest was so broad and the rise so imperceptible that the scene on the other side unfolded itself very gradually. Nevertheless, it was exciting enough and we involuntarily quickened our feeble pace as the first distant blue hills of the Argentine rose above the snow. Then a tiny corner of the lake itself showed almost green against the darker hills, with the long white tongue of the Bismarck glacier projecting far into the water; and at last little by little, far below us, the main glacier unfolded its grey wrinkled mass.

Behind us to the south the ice-cap stretched to the distant rock spires of the Paine region. To the west easy snow slopes led to the summits on the long ridge on which we had gazed for so many days from the other side. To the north rose peak upon peak increasing in height as they became more distant. Most curious, too, was a deep rift in the ice-cap which we could distinguish some ten miles to the north. There, there is only a distance of five miles separating the northern extremity of Peel Inlet from a little lake which was originally an arm of Lake Argentino but is now cut off from it by a glacier. Should this ice barrier melt or break and the little lake become one with its parent, then a mere five miles separates the waters of Lake Argentino from the Pacific Ocean. So far as distance goes this would appear to be the easiest place to cross the ice-cap, but this northern extremity of Peel is long, narrow, choked with ice, and (as the ship's party were to discover) across its entrance is a reef.

Having savoured to the full this wonderful mountain vision we had to decide what to do. From where we were (7,500 ft. above sea-level) what little we could see of the lower Bismarck glacier looked even more tangled and broken than the lower Calvo. On our right the north ridge of Cervantes dropped slowly down to it, to terminate in a high buttress of shaly, yellow rock. At the foot of the buttress the main Bismarck glacier was joined by one almost equally big lying under the east side of Cerro Cervantes. This was fed not only by this mountain but by others further east, and by the ice-cap spilling through the gap in the Cervantes ridge. As we could overlook both glaciers from the buttress we decided to put a camp (Camp IX) on the ridge just short of it.

Owing to either fatigue, excitement, or the tantalising vision of the lake which seemed so near and might yet be so far, I was long in

The Bismarck glacier in contact with the forest about three miles from the lake

going to sleep and woke only when the sun flooded the tent with a yellow light. It was another flawless day as we moved on over the crest and followed the ridge down about 500 ft. to camp on a thin layer of snow overlying a bed of shale. Any idea that we could walk down the main arm of the Bismarck could be dismissed out of hand. Though we might have been able to cross it high up on the *névé*, its northern or true left bank was cut by two formidably fragmented subsidiary glaciers. The other branch, which could be called the East Bismarck, warranted closer inspection. It offered the shortest way to the lake and on its farther side, immediately opposite to our camp, the snow slopes above it gave way to warm, red rock. Could we but reach those rocks there seemed good hopes of our reaching the lake.

That night it began blowing and the morning broke overcast, cold, and windy. A few yards from the tents the ridge fell in precipices to the East Bismarck, but lower down where the buttress sprang up from a col there was a snow ramp leading towards the glacier. What lay between the foot of the snow ramp and the glacier could not be seen, but when we got down we found ourselves groping about in a badly broken icefall. To escape from this we traversed over to some rocks below the buttress and huddled behind them to take stock and to eat our lunch. The weather was deteriorating and a closer view of the glacier, now only about 500 ft. below, was extremely discouraging. Only a short mile separated us from the red rocks, but the sea of ice between broke in tumultuous waves. The only way of reaching the rocks seemed to be to make a long circuit round the head of the glacier on the *névé* and then return along the snow slopes on the far side. As a way of reaching the head of the glacier, the notch in the Cervantes ridge which we had noticed when we first reached the ice-cap at once occurred to us. From where we were the east side of the Cervantes ridge looked impossibly steep. The glacier, however, rose steeply towards its head and might well be accessible from the notch. We would go back and see.

CHAPTER XII

LAKE ARGENTINO AND BACK

Then Alpheus bold
On his glacier cold
With his trident the mountains shook.

SHELLEY

WE WERE ALREADY DISHEARTENED as we toiled back up the 2000 ft. of rock and snow, and then that night we had:

A trifling sum of misery
New added to the foot of our account

when a short but fierce blizzard raged. Although time spent in reconnaissance is never wasted, we felt that this reconnaissance might have been done with advantage from a camp somewhere near the Calvo pass. If instead of blundering on we had stopped and then made a reconnaissance east as well as north some time and strength would have been saved.

Another brilliant morning went far to comfort us as we began the long trudge back over the wide crest. This crest which we had hoped would be the Bismarck Pass we had now christened the Bismarck Saddle, a name which promised nothing and raised no false hopes. Strictly speaking the name Calvo Pass can only be given to the vague shallow depression on the ice-cap which we had reached from the Calvo glacier. If this depression led downwards to the notch, as it did, and if there was a way through the notch down to the East Bismarck glacier, then the name might well be transferred to the notch itself. In that it proved to be narrow and confined between high walls this notch was more like a pass; but it lay several hundred feet below the true pass showing that the Cervantes ridge where the notch lies is not the watershed.

Having traversed back along the ice-cap under the slopes of Cervantes we shed our loads and began to climb. We hoped to be able to reach a point from which we could look down on the notch to see what lay beyond. When we reached the ridge above it we could see that it marked the entrance to a narrow defile leading easily to the glacier below. A short way down the defile was a convenient shelf lying between an ice-fall above and the seracs below. By traversing along this we could reach and cross the glacier where it was reasonably free from crevasses. This route would pass under a black rock spur where we could camp if necessary. Here was the solution of our troubles, the answer to our prayers.

Having retrieved our loads we brewed up. The air was so still that the Primus would burn in the open. Even though the way led downhill we did not reach the notch that evening. Intending to leave two days' food, spare film, and other things on the ice-cap I had picked on a fold in the snow, half cave, half crevasse, still some way ahead of us, as a useful mark. We had neither wands nor flags and as this was the only identifiable feature in an otherwise unbroken expanse of snow it was only wise to take advantage of it. But the snow was soft and deep and we were feeling uncommonly weary so that we made camp 400 or 500 yards short of it. This slackness was to have consequences. Camp X was 6550 ft. above sea-level.

Six days' food seemed ample to take with us—two days to the lake, two days back, and two days in reserve. The rest, enough for two days, together with anything we could leave out of our loads was left behind. This included a great quantity of my exposed film, both colour and black-and-white. As food had also been left at Camp VII on the Galvo side of the pass, and at Camps V and IV, our line of retreat seemed to be secure. We built the dump as high as we could—at least two feet above the ground—and took some bearings.

When we set out for the notch and the red rocks (where we hoped to camp) it was windy and cold. Moving fast over hard snow we were lucky to hit off without hesitation a strait and narrow gate between the ice-fall and the seracs. Skirting under the black rock spur we dropped down to the *névé*-covered glacier and started to cross it, hell-bent on reaching the red rocks which beckoned so invitingly, for we were tired of sleeping on snow. The edge of the glacier close to the snow slopes provided an almost crevasse-free route, but by the time we stepped from soft snow on to dry land in the Argentine, as it were, we were very weary. After some search we found a snug shelf of gravel at the foot of a miniature cliff. Perched a few hundred feet above the glacier this desirable residence boasted a fine view and had water laid on, for a stream trickled down the cliff from a snow bed above. After a fortnight of camping on snow we relished highly the more luxurious warmth of gravel and the abundant water supply. The height of Camp XI was about 4500 ft., the height of Lake Argentino being about 600 ft.

We had now pitched our most distant camp. From here we intended to reach the lake and return to camp in the day. Charles, who had not been able to do much in the way of trail-breaking but had kept going with great determination, decided to take a rest, lake or no lake. For Jorge and me it was Pike's Peak or bust, so we started soon after 5 a.m. on 18 January, carrying only lunch and a camera. At this stage in its journey to the lake the glacier assumed the tortured and riven form we had recognised with some despondency from our view point on the ridge. The *névé* had disappeared and the rough, bare ice close to the rocks was as broken as that of the Calvo. A mile below camp the ice crawled round the foot of a sheer cliff where it seemed more than likely that we might be stopped. We made good progress until we drew near the cliff which we approached along a wet, black gangway of moraine. With enough time one might have made a laborious but more certain route above the cliff, but it would be at a very high level and we were short of time. When ice and cliff met we had to take to the ice which at this point was as black as the moraine it had deposited. We got past the cliff but it was touch and go. A little later in the season, a little more melting, the disappearance of any one of several slender links, and we would have been stopped.

This was the crux. Once the corner had been turned there was nothing to stop us. Round the corner the cliff dwindled to a boulder-strewn slope where a few hardy shrubs struggled for existence and lower down the slopes became more and more forested. While even better for us, far down the glacier the seracs melted away before a grand expanse of flat, dry ice littered with stones and boulders. On we went at a round pace over ice, moraine, or tree-covered bank—which ever was the easiest. At first the forest was of gnarled, stubby, close-growing trees, scarcely penetrable except by following the bed of a fast

The 100 ft. high tongue of the Bismarck glacier projecting into Lake Argentino: This arm of the lake is barely a mile wide and the glacier nearly reaches the far shore; the main body of the lake is some forty miles long and ten miles wide

flowing stream. Lower down it opened out and provided us with good going; but even that was abandoned when we reached the expanse of flat ice over which we sped rejoicing, remarking as we went several fine examples of 'glacier tables'—boulders perched on an ice pedestal. Near the lake this broad highway suddenly broke up into pinnacles and crevasses forcing us back into the shady forest.

The strangest feature of the Bismarck glacier was the proximity of ice and forest, their line of contact being marked by broken branches and fallen trees. The moraine, where it existed, was a ridge a few feet high littered with stripped tree trunks and apparently as fresh as if deposited only recently. At times the ice almost brushed the living trees. We could walk through open forest of tall Antarctic beech on a carpet of yellow violets, while through the trees, only a few yards off, loomed a monstrous wall of ice. Game tracks were plentiful but we saw neither life nor any fresh spoor. In addition to the violets there were purple vetch, berberis, fuschia, a yellow flower like a foxglove, very common in the Central Andes, and a holly-like shrub with a pleasing orange flower which we had often seen on the west side.

The shore of the lake is here so heavily forested that we were denied the blessed sight of its milky blue water until the last moment. It was about noon when in the moment of victory we sank down on the bank for our first halt. The lake itself failed to come up to my high expectation. For one thing we were on a narrow arm so that the opposite shore was barely a mile away. I had hoped to step from the forest on to a grassy sward, graced perhaps by a few flamingos. Instead we sat among nettles and creepers on a steep earth bank, with the water, full of dead branches, about six feet below. In front and on either hand for some way from the shore tops of dead and dying trees rose above the water. Apart from their hindrance to either boating or bathing, to me there is always something peculiarly depressing about black, leafless branches of drowned trees stretched out, as it were, in mute appeal. Still, water is water; and besides my being hot and sweaty enough to make any bathe memorable, here was an occasion—the end of a long pilgrimage over sea and mountain—when not to bathe ceremonially, if need be in boiling spring or ice-bound pool, would have been base indeed. Jorge, with no proud record behind him of ceremonial bathes in far corners of the earth, had no such compelling impulse. Accordingly I rose alone from my bed of briars and nettles, stripped as best I could without getting scratched or stung (there were clouds of virulent horse flies) and bathed. Bathed is, perhaps, an extravagant term for an act which took less than a few seconds to complete; for hard by an ice floe nestled close against the bank.

There were dozens of ice floes and their numbers were being added to at frequent intervals by a thunderous discharge from the glacier tongue which thrusts out into the lake almost as far as the opposing shore. Each ice avalanche was followed by a wave which set the floes rocking on its way towards the shore. This 100 ft. high wall of ice with the sun sparkling on its white pinnacles, with ice caverns a more lovely blue even than the water, looked like a section of the Ross Barrier transported from the Antarctic to the more genial surroundings of hills and forest. Indeed, to anyone ignorant of its parent ice-cap nothing could appear more incongruous than this mass of ice, issuing apparently from the depths of a forest, lapped by the placid waters of a lake, and the whole bathed in brilliant sunshine.

Two hours later we started back. Our slow progress soon made it clear that we should not get back that night. Accordingly before quitting the pleasant open forest we chose a flat spot under the trees with a stream hard by and settled down for the night. Having supped on cold water all we had to do was to collect enough wood for our fire. Dead trees lay in profusion and everything was so dry that we had to be careful not to start a forest fire. In contrast to the forest of the western side this looked as though no rain had visited it for months. Higher up, the mountains of this eastern side must surely receive a great quantity of snow, for the snow line is, perhaps, only a thousand feet higher than on the west.

In the night no strange animals prowled round our camp, no ghastly yell from a Patagonian 'yeti' froze our blood, so that apart from rising frequently to replenish the fire we slept well. Hope, reputedly a bad supper but a good breakfast, was all we had had when, having shaken the leaves from our hair and stamped out the fire, we resumed the march. Although we now knew more of the country and could cut off some of yesterday's corners we found it a weary grind; Jorge, whose breakfast evidently had not agreed with him, lagged behind. But feeling that Charles' anxiety at our absence should not be unduly prolonged I went ahead. Traversing high up on the rocks a mile from camp I saw Charles, with a rucksack bulging with sleeping bags and food, moving slowly down the glacier in search of us. Fortunately I was able to stop him and in the course of the morning the three wanderers foregathered to lie at earth for the rest of the day.

In the night it blew hard, so hard that my tent, inadequately stayed with stones, was uprooted. The wonderful weather of the last few days had broken. When we started in the morning the wind which was already blowing strongly increased as we neared the black rock spur where we meant to camp. It was now a blizzard and we might just as well have camped on the snow where we stood, for the twenty minutes climb to the rocks chilled us to the bone. With numbed hands we struggled to erect the tents in the wholly imaginary lee of the rocks across which the snow drove with stinging force. For the next forty-eight hours the gale beat about us with relentless fury. We were in no condition to sit it out and wait for better times. Our limited food, the uncertainty of reaching and finding our dump, and the now visibly weakening seams of my tent, combined to lower our morale and make us anxious. The Primus, too, either because of lack of air in the tightly sealed tent or because of too much outside, now began to give trouble.

On the morning of Sunday, 22 January, the gale was still blowing and outside it was very thick. We had now only food for that day. We had no choice, therefore, but to get on and find the dump. In addition to the initial difficulty of finding the route and hitting off the extremely tenuous line between the ice-fall and the seracs it seemed possible that beyond the notch the storm might well be worse. At last at midday a glimpse of the sun trying to pierce the flying scud encouraged us to try. The slow, cold job of packing the frozen tents over, we got under way and accomplished the tricky part of the route without a mistake. This was encouraging but beyond the notch driving snow still hid everything. Having little idea beyond a rough compass course where we were going we camped just in time to avoid another blizzard. We thought we were now not more than a mile from the dump and that night we finished our food.

Although in the morning it was still blowing the sun shone through the driving mist and snow. Visibility was from 200 to 300 yards. My plan was to leave the camp standing and search for the dump. This might take a long time to find, for it would probably be covered by the snow of three days of storm. The others were loth to move far away from camp as it was always possible we might not be able to find it again. There was something in that, but there was nothing at all in Jorge's next suggestion, that having no food and little hope of finding any we should retreat to the Argentine. Charles, who was now feeling the cold, agreed with him. This suggestion implied a two-day journey to the lake and then the crossing of some fifty miles rough country before the nearest estancia could be reached.

And all this would have to be done on one tin of biscuits which we had foolishly left at the red rocks. Also, such a decision would impose a severe strain on the ship's party who would have great difficulty in returning through the channels short-handed. I therefore exercised my right of veto and at noon we packed up and started for home. If we found the dump on the way so much the better; if we didn't we could go on to the next, or even the next after that. If we had to go hungry it was better that we should move over country we knew and in the direction of our friends.

Visibility was now less than 200 yards but after an hour's plodding I spotted through the mist the hole where we thought to put the dump but didn't. As compass bearings were of no use in such conditions we had to rely on guesswork for its position. Charles and I, taking different lines, moved off to search, Jorge showing an invincible reluctance to being separated from the loads. As we had only a vague idea where to look we could not waste time prodding the snow; our only chance was that a bit of the dump might still be above the surface. After quartering the ground for some time I reluctantly called the search off. This abandoning of all my exposed film was for me, I think, the bitterest pill, for although the morale of the party was shaken I had confidence that once we were over the pass we should be able to keep going until we found one of the lower dumps.

Nothing was said as we shouldered our loads to move on very slowly. Some way past the hole Charles suggested we should try once more before going too far and I gladly agreed for the mist seemed to be thinning a little. Off we went, Jorge again staying by the loads. Once before Charles' keen eyes had served us in good stead and now he was the first to spot at a distance of 200 yards something very small and black. As I did not wish to rouse Jorge's hopes to no purpose I stifled a whoop of joy and joined Charles as he hobbled towards it. It was the dump all right. We were, indeed, lucky, for only about three inches of the corner of the topmost tin showed above the snow.

Seldom can the finding of pemmican and biscuit have given so much genuine pleasure. For this deliverance from black care we declared a holiday and pitched camp on the spot. Replete with food and tolerably secure in the knowledge that there was more to come, we listened with indifference to the persistent wind. Since the 20th it had been blowing and this extraordinary spell of bad weather proved to be by no means over. Late next morning, the wind having dropped a little, but with visibility of only a hundred yards, we started for the pass steering by compass. As we crossed it in deep powder snow, the mist rolled away revealing the familiar mountains to the west, and we went on down rejoicing to be safely over. Near Camp VII we found ourselves at a loss, for we were unable to recognise the landmarks and could not therefore locate the dump with its two days' food. Had we had to cross the pass without food as was so nearly the case, we should have been in a poor way.

As it was we were not yet out of the wood. Our start was delayed by a blizzard which had blown up in the night, but at 11 a.m. we set off steering by compass, with visibility worse than ever. Much depended on our finding the dump at Camp V but even when the mist did clear we had difficulty in recognising such vaguely remembered landmarks as crevasses or queer-shaped seracs. It was more by luck than anything else that, late in the day, we stumbled on a box sticking out of the snow. For the time being at least we should not go hungry. Camp IV was on unmistakable rocks and at Camp I there was a three days' supply of food, and provided *Mischief* had not miscarried we should be picked up the day after our arrival there.

We looked forward to the short, easy journey between Camps V and IV, and I pictured myself strolling placidly down the glacier, up on to the little col from which we had once looked down into the next valley, and then on to the rocks where we should knock the snow off our boots for the last time. In the event we had a trying day. Starting in mist we continued in mist. All went well until we halted for a snack near the col, but on starting again we missed the route and became deeply involved in a terrible maze. After following a promising line between two crevasses for a quarter mile or so, we would be brought up short by one running transversely. We would then have to retrace our steps and try another only to finish in the same way. Becoming more and more frustrated I at length decided to follow the complicated pattern of our tracks all the way back to the halting place. There we pitched a tent, brewed up, and waited for the mist to clear. When it did we saw our mistake and within an hour had reached camp. It rained all night but that was the last of a seven day spell of very foul weather. Had we met such conditions on the way up I doubt if we ever should have crossed the ice-cap.

We were now faced with a stiff climb over rock and patches of snow for about 2000 ft. before we could begin the downward traverse towards the tree line. Had the weather not taken a turn for the better it would have been a puzzling journey. Instead we had a lovely clear day and enjoyed looking down on our old enemy, the lower glacier, and to Calvo Bay and the Wilcock peninsula beyond. Poor Charles, whose feet for the last few days had been very painful, had a bad time, but he stuck to it nobly. By midday we sat down on a grassy mound just above the tree line to eat our lunch and to select the likeliest point for our attack. We had to drop about 2000 ft. and once the battle with the bush had been joined it would be a case of every man for himself. An hour later, with scratched face and tattered windproofs, I emerged on to the moraine close to Camp II. Jorge followed close behind, and then, *longo intervallo*, the bushes parted and a sort of forest satyr or dryad appeared, leaves in his hair and twigs in his beard. As we foregathered there on the moraine each of us must have looked something like Bunyan's Pilgrim, 'clothed in rags, his face from his own house, and a great burden upon his back'. This final descent through the forest had been a searing experience, creeping under branches, standing on rotten trunks which broke, stepping on to moss hags which had no bottom, slithering down slimy cliffs, dropping like apes from branch to branch, seeing nothing, and able only to go downwards. At one time I had become so firmly lodged in a thicket that I despaired of freeing myself without help. All of us were a little weak.

Down by the shore we pitched our yellow tents on the highest point of the moraine, as a signal, and settled down to wait for the next day but one, Sunday, 29 January. We found two notes which contained bad news. *Mischief* had been aground, had damaged her propeller, and was once again without power. She was anchored in a bay out of our sight some four miles off and we should have to be taken off in the dinghy. On the other hand the promised supply of petrol and paraffin had been delivered. The *Lautaro* (Cmdr. Chubretovich), having failed to find *Mischief* at Puerto Bueno, continued the search in Peel Inlet and finally delivered mail, petrol, and paraffin. Thus, in every sense, the Chilean Navy went out of its way to help us.

CHAPTER XIII

A NEAR THING

Curiosity, like all other desires, produces pain as well as pleasure.
SAMUEL JOHNSON

WHILE JORGE WENT DOWN to the beach to gather mussels, Charles and I collected firewood. If all went well we could expect to be taken off next day; for from the notes left in the pillar-box we learnt that it was their custom for someone to row in on the Saturday, sleep on shore, and then row back on Sunday evening. All the next morning from our look-out on the moraine we played Sister Anne until at last among the distant floes we descried a black speck. Michael with the dinghy arrived in the afternoon, having been rowing and pushing for four solid hours, for the ice was thick. As the dinghy would not hold four men and their kit, we left Charles to be picked up the following day. I took the oars, Jorge acted as bowman with his ice-axe, while Michael conned us from the stern. It was hard work for the dinghy was loaded down to the gunwale, and I was relieved when three hours later we turned the corner and saw *Mischief*'s stumpy mast. In spite of her recent rough handling she looked imperturbably solid and homelike even among such wild surroundings. She lay off a shingle beach where she had been untroubled by wind or ice although the bay lay wide open to the west. It was a happy reunion—a little marred, perhaps, by the occurrences now to be related.

During the row out I learnt why, how, and where *Mischief* had been nearly wrecked. I blamed myself for not having given more explicit instructions that the ship should not be moved unnecessarily, but I never imagined they would want to go swanning about on their own. Enough has been said of the extreme north end of Peel Inlet to show that it must be a fascinating place, and apparently Procter's curiosity to see it proved irresistible. In 1931 Michael Mason had gone nearly as far as the narrow entrance and we knew from his account in *Where*

Tempests Blow that it was full of ice and that a strong current flowed; but it was left for *Mischief* to discover that there was also a bar across it in the shape of a rock reef. Upon this *Mischief* struck, with the result that in this case curiosity produced more pain than pleasure. Once the disaster had happened the small crew, led by Procter, acted with the utmost energy, resolution, and skill, urged on not only by their fear for the ship but also by the knowledge of the consequences that loss or damage to her might have for the party on the ice-cap. Their experience and the anxiety they naturally felt are well described in Michael's own words:

We headed up the north arm of Peel Inlet. It was wide enough to tack against the familiar head wind which later swung right round until we were running at four or five knots with the boom wide out. Ahead the channel bent eastwards with a broad, flat forested swamp on the west bank and steep rock on the other. We kept close in to the rock to avoid possible shallows off the west side, but suddenly we touched. In a moment we were off again having been carried over by, our own momentum. There was no ice about and the channel was still three quarters of a mile wide, and no sign of kelp. Judging it wiser to go no further without investigating, particularly as we could now see round the bend where there were large ice floes apparently aground in the narrowing waterway, we anchored in six fathoms in midstream. Bill Procter and I rowed about in the dinghy sounding to find a better anchorage for the night.

The sound of barks and grunts drew us to a small bay some half mile to the south where we saw some sea lions sunning themselves on a rocky cape. There were twenty to thirty, mostly of a light brown colour, the sun having dried their shiny black skins. The females became uneasy at our presence behind some bushes and presently the huge old bull roused himself. A grunted order and his large family flopped into the sea one after the other in a frenzy of splashing. The bull remained on the rock as a rearguard, his whiskers bristling and his huge body weaving about as he searched the bushes with indignant eyes. Then he, too, took the water, but he was too curious to leave, and swam around, surrounded by his harem, lifting head and shoulders out of the water to get a better look at us.

On returning to the ship we noticed that there was now a strong current and that the ice-floes were being carried down towards us. We weighed at once and headed for 'Sea Lion Bay' which had seemed an excellent anchorage, taking care to keep in mid-stream to avoid the rock we had touched on the way up. All at once, with a lurch and a shudder the boat ground to a standstill—we were hard and fast. I took the kedge anchor off in the dinghy but could make little headway owing to the current. We had not noticed until now how fast the water was flowing, having been deceived by the slack water at high tide. We heaved on the warp but the boat would not budge, and her stern was already high out of the water. It was about 9 p.m. and in the failing light we could make out a boulder-strewn bottom beneath the swirling water.

The topmast was rigged as a leg made fast to the starboard shrouds and took some of the weight as the yacht began to list. Small icefloes drifted on to us, carried at a rate of five or six knots over the reef, and we fended them off as best we could with boat-hook, harpoon, or staysail boom. At two in the morning the water was about two feet deep, rocks were showing above it, and *Mischief* was leaning heavily on the leg. During slack water we spent two hours sounding the length of the reef which extended nearly a thousand yards from shore to shore. The shallowest part was in mid channel where we had struck, and as it extended fifty yards ahead she would have to come off stern first. Near the west bank there was a gap with a depth of one and a half to two fathoms at low water. For one thing we had reason to be grateful—the reef kept off the bigger bergs which had been careering down stream, spinning and breaking up with thunderous roars just before reaching us as they grounded on the edge of the reef. The smaller bergs could be fended off until such time as the stern became too high out of the water for them to be reached. As the tide turned the same bergs came back at us. The bows presented a smaller and less vulnerable target than the stern, but the topmast leg stood out unprotected.

Next morning, 5 January, high water being about 8.30, we laid out the kedge astern but succeeded only in stranding the rope. There was nothing for it but to lighten the ship. Bill rowed ashore with the spare anchor chain and two hundredweight of ballast and landed on a sand spit between two wooded islands 600 yards down stream. I pumped water out of the tanks while John fended off floes. Bill returned towing a stout trunk of Winter's bark which we erected as another leg, and we brought ballast up from the side lockers and put it on the starboard side of the deck to keep her canted as the tide went out. Rowing ashore with five hundredweight of pig iron I nearly sank, as the current was so strong that I could not manoeuvre the dinghy and I got caught up in a whirlpool. Even with the empty dinghy I could not row against the current so that we had to wait for slack water for the next load.

Meanwhile Bill and John, when not fending off ice, took up the cabin tank and floor boards and began levering out ballast and carrying it on deck. This was a back-breaking job and the pigs were hard to grip. At slack water between 2 p.m. and 4 p.m. we got three loads ashore. Each hundredweight pig had to be lowered six feet over the side and a slip would have meant either a holed dinghy or perhaps a broken leg. The boat was now the lighter by a ton of ballast, the spare chain, and about fifteen hundredweight of water. We continued working on the ballast, getting it up first from the port side and putting it on deck in readiness for slack water, one of us keeping iceberg watch and the other two handling the pigs. High water was at 9.30 p.m. We had forgotten about eating but we now lit the fire and put some coffee on. A large berg knocked away both legs, but there was enough water to keep the ship from falling over. The difficulty was to get them back in place with the current sweeping them astern.

We rowed ashore two more loads of ballast. By this time Bill was completely exhausted. He had been a tower of strength, but he had had no sleep for over thirty-six hours and felt the responsibility of the situation. We gave him a sleeping draught and he slept all through the frightful noises of the night, the floes hitting the stern and scraping along the hull. There was a light wind blowing and we were fearful of it increasing and blowing us over. We fixed up the staysail booms on the port side but the ice soon dislodged them. The wind brought the ice down thick and fast. The boathook snapped in my hands as one crashed against the quarter rocking the ship. Others hit the stern and the rudder, and I thought that any moment either this would be smashed or the ship would topple over. Miraculously she withstood the onslaught. By 3 a.m. on the Friday morning the worst was over and we were able to get a little sleep during slack water.

The morning tide brought the ice back and we were now beginning to recognise by their individual shape and size floes as they went back and forth. By daylight, from the dinghy, I looked at the damage. The hull was scraped bare, some of the planking scarred and splintered, the rudder chipped, and the propeller had had one blade chewed to pieces. During slack water we ferried over four more loads of ballast and another three in the afternoon, making a total of sixty-seven hundredweight on shore. 'Ballast Bay' was now littered with pig iron. *Mischief* looked a strange sight stuck out in mid-channel

almost high and dry at low water. It was a beautiful day and we were surrounded by magnificent scenery, but we could not appreciate it.

We cut some more Winter's bark logs and hung them over the stern
weighted with ballast in an effort to protect the rudder from ice. On the ebb
the topmast was again knocked away by ice, but the Winter's bark trunk took
the weight on its own, the boat settling down with a more pronounced list on
this remaining leg. The topmast could not be got back into its hole among
the boulders until low water. In the evening as Bill was taking ashore the
first load of ballast just before high water, without the slightest warning the
bows swung clear and we were off. I took the tiller while John dashed to the
engine, Bill gesticulating madly from the dinghy. We were being carried fast
up stream towards the larger ice floes. John threw the anchor over, forgetting
to pass the chain through the fairlead. However, we were anchored in about
six fathoms close to where we had originally anchored on the Wednesday
evening.

Bill returned and we surveyed the situation. We decided to wait until
low water next morning at about 4 a.m. and then feel our way with the lead
through the gap we had sounded, using the engine at its slowest speed. If
we grounded again we should have a rising tide to float us off. We put the
kedge anchor over and brought up the main anchor and chain with the
handy-billy, for the winch could not be used while the chain was not in its
fairlead. At last all its twenty-five fathoms were got in and then let out again
through the fairlead.

But our troubles were by no means over. On the ebb the ice came down as
before and now we no longer had the protection of the reef against the really
big bergs. For the next five hours Bill stood by the winch letting out chain to
'ride' the blows of the bergs and taking it up again, while I steered against the
force of the current, veering oneway or the other to try to dodge the oncoming ice. From the cockpit I shone the Aldis lamp in accordance with directions
from the bow, and put the tiller over at the last moment to see the huge white
shape glide grudgingly past, scraping the planking and rocking the hull. But
for the biggest this did not work. As the ship swung the mass of ice below
water would catch the anchor chain, tauten it, and drag the ship forward to
collide with a terrifying crash and spray the deck with chips of ice. At times
two bergs would converge on the bows or the bowsprit shrouds, whipping the
spar about almost to breaking point, or an eddy would sweep one round to hit
unexpectedly on the quarter.

When dawn came the tide slackened and *Mischief* was still afloat. We started the engine, weighed anchor, and crept slowly towards the estimated position of the gap, weaving a way through the grounded floes. As I stood in the bows sounding every few yards the suspense was agonising—six fathoms, five, four, three—John standing by the engine ready to go full astern—two-and-a-half, two, two-and-a-half, four, and we were over. We headed for Sea Lion Bay, anchored, and slept for fourteen hours.

On Sunday morning we returned to Ballast Bay during slack tide at high water, and having anchored some seventy yards off shore began rowing off the ballast. We took off the skylight, rigged a derrick with one of the staysail booms, and with the jib halyard and the handy-billy were able to lift the pigs from the dinghy and lower them into the cabin in one operation. We had to get the job done before the next flood tide which would jam the bay full of ice, whereas during the ebb there was none.

The flood tide began running as we weighed, with all the ballast aboard and looking rather lop-sided, preparatory to returning to Sea Lion Bay. Then the worst happened. Just as we came round into midstream the engine stopped. John, cursing wildly, got a few more spluttering revolutions out of it before it failed again. We were being carried back towards the reef. We hoisted sail, but there was not enough wind to stem the tide. Then the engine came to life again making a frightful knocking sound, but we made ground slowly heading in towards the bank where the current was not so strong. The knocking continued and water began pouring in round the propeller shaft. As soon as the engine was switched off the inrush of water subsided to a trickle but we then drifted towards the reef again.

Then the wind freshened. A head wind, but still a wind, and the ship began to gather way heeling over as we hauled in the sheets. Nervously we tacked back and forth, gaining ground each time, and keeping well in midstream until we could fetch Sea Lion Bay. The next morning, with a fresh following wind, we sailed back to the anchorage in *Mischief* cove on the north side of Calvo Bay.

CHAPTER XIV

THE PACIFIC

———◆———

Seamen are cautioned not to make free with these shores as they are
very imperfectly known and from their wild desolate character they
cannot be approached with safety.

CAUTION *(Chart No.24: Channels between the*
Gulf of Trinidad and Gulf of Peñas)

T HE LEAK AT THE INNER END of the stern tube was only serious
if the shaft was revolving. In the opinion of those on board
this had been bent. Later at Valparaiso we found that the bracket
supporting the outer end of the stern tube had been sheered
through. From Michael's account it seems that the ice had almost
sheered through it and then the short time for which the engine
had been running had finished the job, so that the movement of
the unsupported stern tube as the propeller revolved allowed water
to pour in. The noise had no doubt been made by the bent propeller hitting the deadwood. Anyhow we could not run the engine.
Neither *Maipo* nor any other ship could now help us. Only on a
slip where she could be hauled out, or in a dry dock, could this
trouble be cured.

To the north the nearest place with any facilities at all was Puerto
Montt but we doubted whether its resources would be equal to the
straightening of a bent propeller shaft. It was 700 miles away and
Valparaiso, where we had to call for stores and mail and where there
would be no lack of facilities, was only 400 miles further. Another
plan, and probably the best, was to return to Punta Arenas, only 300
miles away, where we could count on the help of the navy. Bound
south, as we should be, we should have better winds and moreover
we knew the anchorages. I inclined to this plan but it would have
involved great disappointment for the others who had set their hearts
on seeing the west coast and making the round of South America.

Without an engine I had strong misgivings about the navigation of the nearly 200 miles of the remaining channels before we reached the open water of the Gulf of Peñas. Among these was the English Narrows, a narrow, tortuous reach about eleven miles long with a five-knot current. In its middle section there is a critical point where steamers have to give a blast on their whistle and may only proceed if there is not an answering blast from an oncoming ship. However, we could avoid this and more than a hundred miles of channel navigation by going out into the Pacific by way of Canal Trinidad which opens off the main channels about sixty miles north of Puerto Bueno. So far to the south we might well meet with rough weather in the Pacific but as long as we could make a good offing we should be all right.

The day after our return, which was wet and windless, Procter went off to collect Charles but did not get back until 6 p.m. Charles went at once to his bunk and remained there until we got to Valparaiso. His foot was in a worse state than I had imagined. One of the toes was in a bad way, the whole foot red and swollen with the poison threatening to spread up the leg. John took him in charge and finally cleared up the trouble by giving his reluctant patient a course of what we called 'bombs'—large tablets of terramycin, sinister yellow in colour, powerful enough to revive the dying and if used to excess to do the living very little good.

When a breeze sprang up after supper we weighed anchor. At midnight the wind died and morning found us over towards the western shore drifting among ice floes. All morning we kept the ice company. Three times we drifted round one enormous floe close enough to have to fend it off, and three times the monster (for which we had by then found a suitable but unprintable name) drifted round us. In the afternoon a fair wind gave us a fast and pleasant sail into and half way up the main branch of Peel Inlet where we were at last clear of ice. Night was closing in when we turned from Peel into Pitt channel, the short cut to the north. That we intended sailing on all night through this narrow, scarcely used channel showed how hardened we had become to channel navigation. But we were also in a burning hurry to get on, and the fact that there was nowhere to anchor was an even more compelling reason. When morning came, bringing with it the typical channel weather of rain and head wind, Pitt Channel looked bleak, gloomy, and lifeless. The shores of Chatham Island on the one hand and the Wilcock peninsula on the other, are steep, rocky, and without much vegetation. A few cormorants were the only sign of life. I had been asked to inspect this east coast of Chatham Island for signs of former Indian habitation, the middens of mussel shells which are often betrayed by the brighter green of the surrounding vegetation; but from the nature of the coast, the absence of coves and the scanty vegetation, it had been of little interest to such people.

The night set in wet and windy when we were still tacking between these two grim walls of rock and making good only about one mile in the hour. At midnight in heavy rain we cleared the dimly seen northern entrance by rounding a high, beetling crag, and turned westwards in Andrew Sound (Seno San Andres). Like Peel, this fjord extends eastwards into the mountains for more than twenty miles. As the weather was becoming very thick, we hove to somewhere between the Kentish Isles and Chatham Island to see what the dawn would bring. The current appeared to run strongly and an unpleasant lop such as would be met in a tide race began breaking around us. Through the mist we could catch fleeting glimpses of high, rocky islands, and while waiting for it to clear, which it did about 8 o'clock, the breeze of anxiety played very strong upon the brow of expectation.

We then had a good run down Seno San Andres to the main channel, which we entered some fifteen miles south of Canal Trindad. In strong and increasing wind we began beating up to Portland Bay at the south-western end of George Island 'a good and convenient anchorage for small vessels'. Just before sundown we could see that we were not going to fetch Portland Bay until long after dark. We could have hove to for the night, for there was room enough, but we had been on the go three nights, Michael and I, Procter and Jorge doing watch about, and we needed rest before beating out to sea by way of Canal Trinidad. On the west side of Canal Concepcion in which we now were, there were on Madre de Dios Island two possible anchorages, Molyneux Bay and Tom Bay, both marked by untended lights. Molyneux Bay lay over on our port quarter so that it would be a broad reach and we might make it while there was still light enough to find our way in.

By this time, with the wind blowing very hard from the north-west, we were sailing with the main reefed, the whole jib, and no staysail.

Running off before the wind we soon romped across to Molyneux
Sound. In addition to the light on the northern entrance there is also
a buoy marking the sunk 'Fawn' rock on which H.M.S. *Fawn* struck in
1870. Leaving the buoy to starboard we had to stand on to the southern shore before going about and heading for the entrance to the bay.
From the bay a wide valley runs inland and down it gusts of wind were
being funnelled with terrible force. Perhaps it was with the hope of
avoiding another tack that I had delayed so long when I put the helm
down only about a cable's length from the rocky shore. *Mischief* came
up into the wind sluggishly, missed stays, and hung there with everything flapping madly. Hoping to wear her round I put the helm up but
with no more success. By the time she was head to wind again we were
drifting backwards. The shore was now only about thirty yards away
and if we went on drifting we seemed unlikely to clear it. The shore
was steep-to, the water deep, and the bottom rocky. In this moment of
crisis Procter ran forward and let go the anchor. More and more chain
ran out—we found the depth was twenty fathoms—but at last to everyone's surprise the anchor took hold and the drift was stopped. Hastily
we hoisted the staysail and shortened the cable. She was yawing about
head to wind, and the moment she paid off on the port tack we let out
the main sheet, wound frantically on the winch, and sailed off with the
anchor and about twenty fathoms of cable dangling below. It had been
a close call, with no one to blame but myself.

Such was the startling prelude to a very dirty night spent hove to
in mid-channel. By morning the wind had dropped but the rain had
increased. It took us four hours to beat back to Portland Bay where we
found good anchorage between two islands.

Canal Trinidad is the recommended way for north-bound vessels
leaving the channels to avoid the English Narrows. As the *Pilot* says:

> The frequent tempestuous weather and heavy seas experienced off
> the western entrance to the Straits of Magellan render the entrance
> into the Pacific by that route at times difficult even for full pow-
> ered vessels. The weather and the sea in Canal Trinidad and its
> offing, about 150 miles northward of the Straits, are generally more
> moderate... It is an excellent channel by which to pass out to the
> Pacific from the Patagonian channels, when the delay occasioned by

Angostura Inglesa will be avoided. The depths in the entrance are
not great, hence there is often a short rough sea even in fine weather.

After our recent alarming experience of beating into an anchorage
under sail alone I was more determined than ever to get into the open
sea; but the forty miles length of Canal Trinidad is open to the Pacific
and since it trends north of west the prevailing wind would raise a big
enough sea to make beating out against it a wearing business. But Canal
Concepcion (we were now lying at its northern end) also leads to the
Pacific, and since it runs west of south we should be sheltered from the
Pacific swell by the islands of Madre de Dios and the Duke of York. We
might even have a fair wind. The distance to the open sea was shorter
this way, but we should enter it a degree further south in lat. 52° S.

After considering both routes we decided in favour of Canal Concepcion. We spent a wet morning renewing the rope tails of the wire
topping lifts, repairing jib sheets, and clearing the deck of the useless oil drums. There is a peculiar satisfaction to be had in throwing
things overboard and the bigger they are the better. The jettisoning of
two forty-gallon drums of petrol was, I felt, a magnificently large ges-
ture which gave me great pleasure at a time when pleasures were rare.
As it was unlikely that we should be putting into any more Patagonian anchorages we collected a lot of mussels and began a futile hunt
for duck. At 2 o'clock in light wind and rain we got our anchor and
headed south-west. Off Moraine Island we streamed the log, as though
we were already in the ocean.

By evening the wind had headed us (we thought this spiteful, for
we were sailing south) and the night was spent beating into sharp hail
squalls. As we forgot to take in the log it had fouled the propeller as
we had gone about and was never recovered. The day continued in like
fashion and by evening we were wondering whether to take shelter for
the night—though none of the available coves looked inviting—when
the sky cleared and the wind veered so that we could lay the course.
Hardening our hearts we pressed on to the south-west. Early in the
morning we were about five miles south of Gape Ladrillero, the southernmost point of the Duke of York Island. Now there was no land to the
west of us nearer than New Zealand, and even that was further north.
The wind was fresh, the sky cloudy, and a big swell was running, but

since on the other tack we could steer no better than north we held on south-west. At all costs we must get away from the coast. The weather thickened and soon we had seen the last of Cape Ladrillero. As the day advanced the wind increased to gale force bringing with it heavy rain and high seas.

This was the sort of rude welcome we had expected from the Pacific in this latitude. Jorge, who was now having his first experience of rough weather took to his bunk and stayed there; and that night I took his watch though feeling far from happy. Charles was already *hors de combat* and now John retired from the scene, too ill to cook. His illness was puzzling since he had never suffered before in bad weather, and it was not until Charles, turning over in his mind the theory of medicine, had recommended quinine, that he began to recover. Apparently it was a recurrence of malaria which he had contracted in Malaya when a prisoner of war. It could not have happened at a worse time than in these few days of storm and stress when only three of the crew were available both for work on deck and for the necessary cooking below.

Having already reefed right down, at midnight we hove to on the starboard tack; but early on the morning of 6 February the wind began to moderate and by midday we were under all plain sail. We were still on a W.S.W. course and the log—for we had streamed our spare— showed fifty miles run since our last sighting of Ladrillero. During the night the wind backed and for the first time allowed us to make some northing. But the weather was by no means settled. Another gale blew up, compelling us to reef closely and also to put about, for we were being driven towards the land. If *Mischief* has a fault, it is a reluctance to go about in heavy weather. At the third attempt we got her round, but once more the log line wrapped itself round the propeller.

This was our worst night. Because we were tired and short-handed we fought shy of getting the mainsail off and therefore hove to with it reefed right down instead of setting the storm trysail. But the task thus shirked had to be done in the end and then under worse conditions. In the early hours of the morning the leach of the mainsail split and it had to come down. Having stowed and lashed the sail we handed the storm jib and lay under bare poles in the trough of the sea, pointing southwest, thus trying to lessen the drift to the south-east.

Mischief lay there quite happily, taking each wave as it came and shipping very little water. Only occasionally when she was obliged to kick her stern high in the air was her dignity at all ruffled, for she is a wholesome seaboat. The happiness of the crew was less noticeable. Snugged down as she was, with nothing aloft to come adrift, we had no anxiety for the ship; nevertheless the fury and violence of the storm were intimidating. One's eyes became inured to looking out over a wild, angry waste of water; to watching the tumult of seas upon the horizon; and to seeing a wave rear high above the ship to break a few yards away and rush harmlessly by. But it was less easy to withstand the constant uproar—the steady menacing whine of the wind as it tore through the rigging, rising with each gust to a fierce scream; the mournful undertone of protesting creaks and groans from the ship; and the sinister hiss of waves as they broke and creamed by under the lifted counter.

Short-handed as we were and faced by a prospect of repeated north-westerly winds or gales it seemed to me doubtful whether we should be able to beat northward into more genial latitudes. To make any northing at all we had first to bend the spare mainsail, for she would not work to windward under the trysail. I began toying with the idea of hoisting the trysail and running south in order to reach the Atlantic by way of Cape Horn. The stores awaiting us at Valparaiso were of little importance and now that we were in open water the repair of the propeller could wait. In fact, so long as we did not have to go through the Panama Canal it could wait until we got home. But neither Procter nor Michael cared much for this idea and in the event they were right. We agreed to struggle on for at least three or four more days hoping for a favourable slant of wind before finally committing ourselves to the daunting prospect of rounding Cape Horn.

Meanwhile, we had very little idea of how far off or rather how near the coast was. The wind had been mostly from northwest and as the set in this latitude is easterly, I was fearful that we might sight land to the east at any time. In the course of the morning the weather improved and the sun came out. The rough and ready noon sight which I got put us in lat. 51°30'S. not so far south as I had expected. The deck watch had not been checked for many weeks; indeed, since leaving Punta Arenas we had, more than once, forgotten to wind it, for there was no need to take sights in the channels. The charging engine had broken down and the battery was flat so that we could not get time signals. Sights, therefore, were no help in finding our longitude, but by taking the sun when it was on the meridian (which we could find by trial) we could at least find our latitude. When we had reached the latitude of Valparaiso we would close the land.

In the afternoon we began sailing under trysail and storm jib on a south-westerly course. Our most urgent task was to unbend the torn mainsail. Working on the reeling deck with the wet, heavy canvas was not easy, but by evening we had the sail folded in an unwieldy heap and lashed it on top of the deck water tank between the cabin skylight and the companion way. Next day the wind was still north-west and the sea still ran high, but the sun was shining. The spare mainsail, a brand new sail, had to be got up from its home in the galley. It took three men to lift it. Jorge, who had now got his sea legs, took the helm while the three of us pushed it by main force through the cabin door and out on to the deck. When we stopped for lunch it was bent and ready for hoisting and in the afternoon it went up to the cheers of the crew. A fine sight it was—this great spread of new white canvas. We unreefed the staysail, hoisted the working jib, put the ship about, and steered north.

All night—the stars showing for the first time for many days— we steered north with a moderate breeze and a lumpy sea. In the morning, Procter poking about hopefully under the counter with our home-made gaff retrieved the log-line with the rotator still on it. The quite unexpected recovery of this useful instrument, the weather, and above all the northerly course, had a wonderfully cheering effect, and our satisfaction in watching the steady climb of the barograph needle was checked only by the thought that what goes up must come down. A week had passed since we had reached the open sea and now at last we began to reel off the miles northwards. On the first day sixty-four miles, rising to 144 on our best day, and averaging ninety-two for the twelve days between the recovery of the log and our arrival at Valparaiso.

Now that we could look forward to fine and increasingly warm weather, fair winds, and a good kick from the Humboldt current, we could heartily congratulate ourselves on not having attempted to go south about. John was up and about, only poor Charles remained prone, barely able to put his bad foot to the ground. Our felicity was only a little marred by the absence of electric light. In the cabin we used an oil lamp but the binnacle had to be lit with a slow-burning carriage candle. As one candle did not quite last the night the man on watch had to change it, a tricky job when we were running before the wind, when he could only leave the helm for a matter of seconds.

In these latitudes in the Pacific there seemed to be less life than in the Atlantic. We saw neither fish, porpoises, nor whales. Albatross of various kinds were the commonest birds. Many of them were immature. There is a striking difference between the sight of an albatross in majestic flight and an albatross resting on the water. Family parties of four or five used to sit in a close circle facing each other, and looked comically frumpish and dowdy. They seldom followed in the wake of the ship, but preferred sitting on the water to watch us go by and after a due interval flying ahead of us to settle down for another look.

The Humboldt current which flows northwards up the coast from about lat. 43°S. nearly to the equator, did not give us the boost we had expected. The air became daily warmer but owing to this cool current the water temperature remained at about sixty degrees. We started bathing again and shed our long Patagonia underpants. Every day we had been expecting to raise the coast but we must have been much further west than we reckoned. However, when a meridian altitude put us in lat. 33°3'S. we set a course for the Punta Angeles light on the south side of Valparaiso Bay, and on the night of 23 February, a fine moonlight night, picked it up dead on the bow. At dawn when the light was close abeam the wind failed and fog came down. We lay becalmed in the midst of a fleet of small, open boats busy fishing off the edge of a reef running north-west from Punta Angeles. Our arrival had evidently been noticed by the lighthouse keeper before the fog closed down, for an imaginative newspaper reported us as 'drifting helpless and exhausted in the last extremity of thirst'. All morning, while the foghorn boomed from the lighthouse, we were a source of free entertainment to the fishermen as we lay waiting for someone to give us a tow. Finally, one of them took Procter ashore and soon after a harbour launch came out, towed us in, and left us in splendid isolation tied to an enormous buoy.

CHAPTER XV

VALPARAISO TO THE PANAMA CANAL

***

Many thousand miles behind us
Many thousand miles before

SEA CHANTY

VALPARAISO BAY, edged for half its length by the city and backed in the distance by the Cordillera, is a fine piece of water. Unluckily it is open to the north, a quarter from which in winter some fierce storms blow. There is an inner harbour where big ships may lie protected by an outer wall; but when a norther blows waves sweep over the wall and the swell makes the quay side untenable. The bay is so deep that the prolongation of the outer wall to gain further protection would be a vast undertaking. Looking at the town from the bay one wonders how it got its name. It lies along the foot of a high ridge, straggling a little way up the slopes. There is not any sign of valley and not the vaguest resemblance to paradise. One wonders, too, where the busy part of the town lies, for there appears to be nothing between the water front and the half-finished streets which peter out on the arid slopes behind. On landing one finds that the business and shopping centres are strung out for a mile or more along a narrow strip of flat ground at the foot of the slopes, and that this is connected by lifts with the steep residential quarter. At least this used to be the residential quarter, but the most favoured spot now is Vina del Mar, a few miles north along the coast.

For several days we lay alongside the outer wall among the fleet of small trawlers. The harbour is filthy and very soon the ship, the warps, and even our clothes were covered with a film of black oil. Later we anchored off the Yacht Club. Here the water was equally dirty and although we saved our warps we had to use the dinghy to go ashore so that that became smeared with oil. The dinghy caused some amusement. It was clinker built and after its bashing in the ice each plank had long whiskers of wood fibre sticking from it, so that when we had it bottom up on the deck preparatory to painting, an interested onlooker asked if we were going to shave it. The Yacht Club shared its premises with the rowing clubs—British, German, Italian, French, Chilean. The city fire service, by the way, is organised on similar lines. Each of these communities runs a voluntary fire brigade, and the rivalry in smartness of turn-out and efficiency is intense. Of the three activities—rowing, putting out fires, and yachting—the last seemed the least popular. Owing to what seem to be rather grandmotherly restrictions, yachting in Chile does not flourish. Unless the owner or skipper of a yacht has a certificate of competency in navigation and seamanship, for which he must pass an examination, he cannot take his boat more than a few miles from the harbour. The result is that there are very few sea-going yachts.

The British consul (Mr Dobson) put himself to endless trouble on our behalf, and both he and the director of the Institute Chileno Britanico (Mr Grant Robertson) extended great hospitality. Through the consul I got in touch with Lloyd's surveyor (Mr James Dobbie D.S.C.) who arranged for *Mischief* to go into the floating dock. This dock has a remarkable history. In our edition of the *South America Pilot* (1941) it figures as 'reported sunk and will probably become a total loss'. During a norther the dock did capsize and sink with a ship inside (the dock is 350 ft long); the ship remained on the bottom, but the dock was raised by her present owner (Señor Corsson), the head of a large ship repair yard. As there are no slipways capable of taking small fishing boats or large yachts, these are often hoisted out of the water by crane. There was a crane capable of lifting *Mischief*, but even if the inside ballast was first removed the hoisting of her on a couple of slings might well have strained her.

Mischief in company with three large trawlers was not due to go into dock until mid-March, so we had time on our hands. Apart from the sending up of the top mast, painting the deck, and having the charging engine put right, there were no major jobs to be done. This enabled the crew, in turns, to spend a few days in Santiago. Here we were able to visit Jorge in his home, and also from the comfort of a car belonging to the Hon. H. A. Hankey of the British Embassy to see something of the peaks and glaciers of the Central Andes at fairly close quarters. Charles betook himself to a hotel for according to the doctor's report it did not seem likely that he would be able to finish the voyage in *Mischief*. Michael spent a lot of time at the Seamen's Institute, not so much because of the seamen who frequented it as the several kindly disposed girls who on certain evenings offered their services as dancing partners in the hope of keeping seamen away from the less reputable places. The Institute was presided over by a Mr Henry Boys, a Yorkshireman who had spent most of his life in Chile and who did us many kindnesses.

In due time we entered the dock in the wake of the three German trawlers. The dock rose, and *Mischief* was high and dry. Her propeller shaft was taken to the workshop and found to be undamaged; only the propeller blades needed welding and aligning. The hull was in surprisingly good order, almost free from weed and barnacles, but we used the opportunity to have it scraped and repainted with antifouling paint kindly given to us by a shipowner (Señor Alfredo Gubbins). The dock superintendent contributed paint for her topsides, so that *Mischief* emerged from the dock looking most raffish with bright yellow topsides and a dark green underbody. The dock-master, Mr Blatt, a Rumanian refugee who had once been master of a vessel, was a genial soul and well disposed towards us. He liked the British. This was all the more strange because we had not been able to do much for him in return for his war-time services to us in the Mediterranean. It was, I fear, a consequence of this preference that the bill for painting *Mischief* must unwittingly have been paid by the owners of the German trawlers which were having their hulls scraped and painted at the same time. Mr Dobbie superintended the refitting of the shaft and the propeller, and thanks to his good offices and the generosity of the owner of the dock we paid nothing whatever for its use or for the repairs which in all fairness should have cost us a very large sum. Such are the extraordinary kindnesses which visiting yachtsmen receive in foreign parts.

On Friday, 23 March, after five days in the dock we motored out and tied up to a buoy. We were now ready for sea and only waited for a young Chilean, George de Giorgio, who was to come with us to England in place of Charles. He had been in his father's yacht as far as the South Seas and the Florida coast and was therefore an experienced sailor. He lived at the small fishing port of Quinteros on the other side of the bay from us, and as at one time I had thought of going there to pick him up I had put Quinteros on our clearance papers as our immediate destination. After his name had been put on our crew list he found his passport needed renewing. Chilean officialdom refused to be hurried. In spite of threats by George's father of speaking to the President himself by telephone, the port authorities struck his name off our crew list. I was determined to sail that day. Postponement meant making out a fresh lot of papers and I was heartily sick of Valparaiso and the attendant troubles of a long stay in port.

I gave George until 5 o'clock to see what he could do. When the hour came we started hoisting sail but, luckily for George, we were unable to cast off as Mr Dobbie was still on board. He had come to say good-bye and his launch had broken down half-way between ship and shore. The launch finally came alongside at the same time as did another carrying the excited George. He had got his passport, but as the port office had closed he had not been able to have his name restored to the crew list. All this bother had aroused some interest. A port official came with him in the launch to see that there was no funny business, so I dared not take him with us from Valparaiso. I, therefore, made a hasty arrangement to pick him up at Quinteros and told him to expect us at midnight.

On the south side of Quinteros Bay there is a high promontory with a lighthouse. Approaching this just before midnight we saw the headlights of a car climbing the steep road to the lighthouse. George's father was evidently on the look-out, so we gave him a signal with our Aldis lamp for we had no lights showing. Having rounded the cape and entered the small harbour we heard the chug of an engine. A launch appeared out of the night, a kit bag was flung on board, and George followed. Still under way, we turned and headed out to sea.

The run to Callao, a distance of some 1200 miles, was done in eleven days. The first day was remarkable in that we sighted a solitary sperm whale and also the snows of Aconcagua about 110 miles away. After our long stay in port both Michael and I were sea-sick. We started promisingly with a fresh southerly wind and in a few days we picked up the south-east trades. We hoisted the twins and bowled along at six knots, while *Mischief*'s tiller gave little shivers of delight, like a favourite dog waiting for a walk. But owing to the cool Humboldt current we had not the sparkling seas and the radiant days such as we had delighted in, in the north-east trades. The sky remained obstinately overcast. Neither was it 'flying-fish weather'. Apart from one solitary monster weighing a good ¾ lb. which came over the stern on the second night, we caught none and saw few. A less welcome visitor was a rat which had evidently joined the ship when we were in dock. We heard him moving about at night and later we found a large hole eaten in the Genoa and the beginnings of a nest. A night or so later we trapped him.

We were well out to sea now and the few sea birds we saw were essentially albatross and the little black storm petrels, but soon an increasing number of cormorants told us that we were approaching the Peruvian coast. This is rich in bird life, particularly so around the Chincha Islands where there are great guano deposits. When we saw the first cormorants we must have been still a hundred miles from land. I took particular note of the distance because of a reference to cormorants in the *South America Pilot*. Referring to the approach to the Falkland Islands it says: 'Penguins may be seen and heard as much as 300 miles from land; they need not, therefore, cause any alarm; the presence of cormorants, however, is well worth noting, as these birds are rarely seen more than ten miles offshore'.

We began to see birds in undreamt-of numbers. There were many types of gulls but in particular cormorants and pelicans. In the air they looked like trails of smoke or swarms of locusts and when they settled their multitudes covered many acres of sea. More than one cormorant landed on our deck to stay for half an hour or more preening his feathers and allowing himself to be fondled as well as photographed. The pelicans were quite as ludicrous as were the steamer ducks. Long strings of them zoomed past us in single file, their heads and beaks drawn back and chests thrown out, suggesting a file of slightly pompous city aldermen. To settle on the water they merely folded their wings and did a sort of belly-flop sending up a cloud of spray. Their take-off was equally clumsy. In addition there were penguins and vast numbers of boobies or gannets. The latter are always worth watching, particularly when making their spectacular dives. In his book *Autobiography of a Bird-lover* Dr F. M. Chapman gives a graphic description of the bird life in these waters, and of a remarkable 'barrage of boobies' which he witnessed:

As for the birds, who can describe them in their incalculable myriads? Visible link in the chain of life that begins with diatoms nourished by the cool, highly oxygenated waters of the Humboldt current, they animate both the sea and the air. No other coastline of similar extent can show an avian population equalling that of Peru.

On 28 November 1918, off the port of Salaverry where my Red Cross mission had taken me, whichever way one looked from our anchorage, birds could be seen in countless numbers fishing in dense excited flocks, passing in endless files from one fishing ground to another, or massed in great rafts on the sea.

Seaward, like aerial serpents, sinuous files crawled through the air in repeated curves, while low over the waters processions passed rapidly, steadily, hour after hour, with rarely a break in their ranks during the entire day. At times the flocks were composed of cormorants; at others they were composed of white-bodied, brown-winged boobies.

When the birds stopped to feed, the scene commanded the attention of every passenger aboard the ship. The cormorants fished from the surface in a sea of small fry. Swimming and diving, they gobbled voraciously until their storage capacity was reached. Then they floated in dense black masses waiting for the process of digestion to give space for further gorging.

The boobies fished from the air, plunging into the water with great force from an average height of 50 ft. to disappear in a jet of spurting spray as they hit the surface. In endless cataracts they poured into the sea. It was a curtain of spearheads, a barrage of birds.

In certain years a warm, southerly counter-current flows down the coast of Peru raising the temperature of the water by ten degrees and more. This is enough to upset the generally stable oceanic conditions. The fish and most of the small living organisms associated with cool waters, die, and great numbers of birds die or migrate in consequence. Sharks, tropical dolphins, flying fish, and jumping mantas or giant rays, appear in waters where they are never normally seen. Associated with the phenomenon of the warm current is another known as the 'Callao Painter', a sulphuretted emanation from the sea which darkens the white paint of ships and tarnishes the silver in houses close to

The friendly cormorant which came on board off
the Chincha islands

John with a 'dorado' which he had just caught

the shore. It is thought to be caused by the death of vast numbers of organisms which then give off the gases of decomposition.

The infrequent influx of this warm current (known locally as Corriente del Nino, because it usually begins about the time of Christmas) seriously affects not only the fishing but also the guano industry. The story of the exploitation of the guano deposits on the Chincha Islands is told in Murphy's *Ocean Birds of South America* and is of interest. The remarkable effect of guano as a fertiliser was known to the Incas and to their Spanish conquerors. Early in the nineteenth century, as it was not found elsewhere, it became one of the chief exports of Peru. In 1840 only twenty barrels were brought to England, but a few years later, when the earlier prejudice to it had been over-come, it was in general use and the guano trade had become a huge commercial interest. In 1847 an official Peruvian survey put the deposits on the Chincha Islands at some twenty-three million tons, the depth of the deposit being fifty-five metres. At the estimated rate of consumption these deposits would last 170 years. Six years later the deposits had been reduced to a mere eight million tons and the sales of guano accounted for more than half the total revenue of the Peruvian government. In 1860 no less than 433 large sailing ships loaded guano at the Chinchas and before 1870 the deposits were worked out. It was a time when 'guano fever burnt as fiercely as gold fever, when the Chinchas were a focus of greed and corruption; a centre of dust-gagged misery and slavery as well as of important business ventures represented by calculating Yankee and British sea captains, and by costly ships with towering spars'. At that time the guano was dug by coolies who sweated out their lives on these barren, rainless islands under the lashes of black overseers. Guano is now, as then, a government monopoly, but the working of it is carefully controlled, each island being taken in rotation after a two to three years' rest. The amount taken out annually is about a quarter million tons.

On the evening of 4 April Isla San Lorenzo on the south-west side of Callao Bay appeared on the bow. With a leading wind we had another glorious moonlight sail round the north end of the island and across the wide bay. The usual difficulty of sorting out sea and shore lights and identifying the harbour lights, was not made any easier by the absence of an important red-flashing buoy at the entrance to the channel. Moving slowly up the channel with the sea wall close on our starboard hand, we saw at last the masts of a great fleet of yachts and we anchored outside them in six fathoms at 3 o'clock in the morning. The noise of our cable running out woke two fishermen in a rowing boat, who now discovered that their net was wrapped round *Mischief*'s bows. This premature hauling of their net proved quite fruitful, and after disentangling ourselves we bought some fish.

Callao is merely the port for Lima, the capital, which lies eight miles inland. We arrived early on the Thursday morning and we left on Saturday evening, the shortest and least troublesome stay of any we had had. Would that they had all been like that! In duty bound we went up to Lima, Pizarro's 'City of the Kings'. There is an electric tramway to it but the better way is to take a taxi. One merely piles in and the taxi leaves as soon as it is full. No one thinks of taking a taxi to himself.

The climate of Lima is not attractive. According to the guidebook rain rarely falls, but it might have added that the sun rarely shines. For more than half the year the weather is dull, and considering the latitude, only twelve degrees south of the equator, uncommonly cool. On many days there is a fog almost as wetting as rain, and on the day of our visit rain fell heavily. All this cloud and fog is attributable to the cool Humboldt current. Possibly on a clear sunny day, when the neighbouring foothills and the high Andes are both visible, the first city of South America might appear worthy of its setting. For some reason I could never accustom myself to thinking of South American towns as old; yet the Lima Cathedral was begun before Henry VIII died. It was founded by Pizarro and in one of the chapels is a glass vase containing what are believed to be the bones of that fierce conqueror. Fires, earthquakes, and wars, civil and foreign, have not left much of the old architecture and what has taken its place is not remarkable.

So far as trade and currency go Peru is free, like Uruguay, but for those bold spirits who think or say that such freedom is not enough accommodation is found in a prison on Isla San Lorenzo. Near the quay there was a combined tobacco and trinket shop, with a 'cambio' which would change our traveller's cheques for dollars over the counter; whereas to cash a cheque in a South American bank was a lengthy operation which seemed almost to necessitate calling a board meeting.

On Saturday we came alongside the Club landing stage for water, petrol, and the fresh stores we had ordered. In view of the belt of calms north of the equator and the calms which at that time of year before the rainy season prevail in the Gulf of Panama, we expected to use the engine a lot. In addition to the full tanks, therefore, we took a drum on deck, but after we had lashed it down we discovered a leak. It was a Saturday afternoon and there was no finding the supplier in order to get it changed. But a stranger standing on the Club steps came to our rescue; drove me round Callao in his station waggon until we found a sound drum, and then would not let me pay for it. He turned out to be a Dutchman who had left Holland as a youth in the first World War and was now a missionary among the Indians.

Quite a large crowd had gathered on the landing stage to see us start. There seemed to me to be more than an even chance of our giving a repeat performance of what had happened at Punta Arenas on a Saturday afternoon; nevertheless, we were determined to leave behind a favourable impression of our seamanship by sailing out. We were lying alongside the stage head to wind with only a few yards of deep water between our bow and the sea wall, the way out running parallel to the wall and down a narrow lane bounded on the other side by a line of moored yachts. We made the mistake of not hoisting the jib as well as the staysail and mainsail. When we cast off and pushed the bow out she began forging ahead rather quickly instead of paying off, so that when she finally did swing round the stem missed by inches the blocks of concrete sunk at the foot of the wall. The shrill warning cries from the landing stage were superfluous, for what might happen was all too clear. But we held on, outwardly calm, as though such delicate manoeuvres were a matter of course with us. *Mischief* did not fail, and with gathering speed she bore away down the channel.

North of Callao sailing should be pleasantly quiet. Gales are almost unknown, the weather is variable enough to keep interest alive, and the heat is not oppressive. Since gales are not expected one becomes, perhaps, a little careless, so that once again we managed to blow out the clew of the Genoa by carrying it at night. We found more life in the sea here than in the corresponding latitudes in the Atlantic. Whales were often seen and one big sperm whale surfaced so close to the ship that his spout covered us with spray. The sight of seagulls perched on what looked like small rocks was a little disturbing until we found they were standing on the backs of turtles. We caught a dorado and lost two more while trying to get them on board. George harpooned a squid. This was the ugliest creature imaginable, with a horny parrot beak, prominent eyes, and ten long arms with suckers on the under side. The two longest arms are used for grabbing his prey while the other eight serve the purpose of knife, fork, and spoon. He weighed about 60lb. Off Cape Blanco we went close inshore in the hope of catching a really big fish, for these waters are reputed to be the best in the world for big game fishing. The largest fish ever caught on a rod, a black marlin weighing 1135lb., was caught here in 1952. Except for a prolific growth of oil derricks and oil tanks the coast hereabouts is barren.

Longer periods of calms, thunderstorms, and heavy rain, heralded our approach to the Gulf of Panama. When we were still sixty miles from land numbers of swallows and dragon-flies came on board. On 24 April we sighted Cape Marzo, a bold rugged headland on the eastern side of the entrance to the gulf. A strong current sets in here, circles the head of the gulf as if in a basin, and then flows out southwards past the western entrance. We drifted thirty miles in the course of the night and spent a jolly day drifting and sailing northwards with the Pearl Islands close on our port hand. As pearl fisheries the islands once rivalled those of Bahrein in the Persian Gulf. They looked like a beach-comber's paradise—waving palms, little beaches of dazzling white sand, and the warm blue water gently lapping a shore 'where slumber is more sweet than toil, than labour in the deep mid-ocean'.

Once they were visited by men of very different ideas. They brought to my mind *Westward Ho!* which opens with John Oxenham and Salvation Yeo busy recruiting men for a wild adventure which so nearly succeeded. Oxenham had been Drake's second in command when they captured the treasure train in Darien, when together they had looked out upon the Pacific and prayed that God would give them leave and life to sail upon it in an English ship. In this great resolve Oxenham anticipated Drake by three years. In 1575, having made the coast near Nombre de Dios in a ship of 140 tons with a crew of seventy, he concealed the ship with branches of trees and marched inland with all the men dragging two small cannons. On reaching a river that ran into the Gulf of Panama they built a 45ft. pinnace, sailed into the gulf, and landed on one of the Pearl islands. They got very few pearls but after lying in wait for ten days they took a small bark from Peru laden with a staggering sum of gold. 'When you strike oil, stop boring' is a sound maxim, but Oxenham was not satisfied. In a week they took another ship laden with silver bars, but by then the hornet's nest had been properly stirred. News of their activities had reached Panama and a strong force was out looking for them. The story goes that the Spaniards discovered the river Oxenham's men had followed by the number of hen's feathers floating down! The Spaniards recovered the bulk of the treasure while Oxenham and his men were away relaying part of it to their ship. An attempt to retake it was beaten off with heavy loss and meanwhile another party of Spanish soldiers from Nombre de Dios found the ship. In the end all the Englishmen were either killed or taken, Oxenham himself being sent to Lima for judgment. There, after frankly admitting that this was a piece of private enterprise and that he had not the Queen's license, he was executed. Whatever their motive, love of fame, greed of gold, lure of discovery, or hatred of Spain and its religion, the Elizabethan seamen possessed boundless hope, courage, self-reliance, and endurance, of which the like has never since been seen.

After rounding the northernmost island we met a strong breeze from the west and beat up against it till nightfall when we raised the lights of Balboa. Motoring on past a number of ships waiting to enter the canal we were presently picked up by the beam of a searchlight and stopped by a launch. We followed this to an anchorage where the port health officer boarded us. Having nothing else to do he sat yarning until 2 a.m. and we were not sorry when the arrival of another ship called him back to duty. In the morning, after *Mischief* had been measured for canal dues, we tied up at a wooden jetty while I went to the canal offices to pay. Having parted with the modest sum of thirteen dollars I got back to the ship just as our canal pilot arrived, whereupon we cast off and followed a German steamer the eight miles to the Miraflores locks.

Steamers are hauled in and out of the locks by electric 'mules' and are held in the middle by six wire warps, but a comparative mite like *Mischief* merely lies alongside the lock wall, the mast barely showing over the top and the crosstrees almost scraping it. As the water enters the lock there is a considerable surging and the pilot had to watch our bow and stern lines carefully while we stood by to ease or tighten them. We also kept the engine running. The two Miraflores locks raise a ship fifty-four feet to the Miraflores lake. We had to wait here pending the arrival of a south-bound ship which was being towed. (The canal, of course, trends from south to north, or slightly west of north, and not from west to east as one might expect). While waiting we housed the bowsprit—that is, we ran it in board— and it was well we did. The Pedro Miguel lock a mile further on raises the water thirty-one feet to the level of the Culebra Cut, the highest level reached, eighty-five feet above sea-level. In this lock we surged about so much that the bowsprit would certainly have been damaged had we not housed it. All the lock gates are doubled as a precaution against ramming, and in front of them is a heavy chain which sinks as the gates open and automatically arrests or slows down a ship that is travelling too fast. In addition the locks themselves are duplicated.

The eight miles long Culebra Cut debouches into Gatun lake, an artificial lake covering an area of 164 square miles on whose surface half submerged hillocks and trees can be seen. We crossed it in the dark, the channel being so well lit, with pairs of leading lights at the bends, that it was like motoring up Piccadilly. Our pilot paced up and down our twenty feet of deck space like a caged lion, urging us to give her all we could. We did our best but *Mischief*'s speed under power is only four to five knots and it was midnight before we reached Gatun, hours behind the last north bound ship. So we anchored for the night and our pilot went ashore to sleep in an air-conditioned room. Steamers pass through the lake at eight to ten knots, the whole transit taking seven hours from Balboa to Cristobal.

Having taken on an Atlantic side pilot we got under way about noon when the first of the ships from the Pacific entered the lock. There are three locks at Gatun to lower a ship the eighty-five feet to the Atlantic. As we descended the surge did not seem so strong as when we had been raised, but as we left the lowest lock the powerful currents demanded full use of the helm to prevent *Mischief* being swept to the side. At Cristobal, six miles from the locks, we moored off the Yacht Club among a number of other sea-going yachts, some of them bound on long passages. There was an Austrian in a double-ender bound for the South Seas single handed who, as we heard, had made a spectacular arrival. Disdaining to anchor, he had jumped overboard and swum ashore with his mooring warp. There were also two young Englishmen in a 21ft. sloop called *Skaffie* which had been badly damaged when crossing the Atlantic. They were bound for New Zealand but owing to shortage of funds for repairs they contemplated giving up the voyage and selling her.

CHAPTER XVI

ROLLING HOME

The bunks were hard and the watches long,
The winds were foul, the trip was long.

'LEAVE HER JOHNNY' SEA CHANTY

A LTHOUGH CRISTOBAL is in the canal zone one has merely to cross a road to reach Colon in Panama. I think it is probably worth while to cross this road occasionally just for the sake of exchanging clean, quiet propriety for bustling life and rowdy squalor. In Cristobal one might as well be in a well-planned garden city in Utopia, only without any shops. In Cristobal the tourist can only buy stamps whereas in Colon there is pretty well everything except rotators for patent logs. George bought a very fine green-eyed stuffed alligator which he polished assiduously with brown boot polish all the way home.

Since we did not expect to reach England before 1 July, by which time Michael's leave would have expired, he had to go home by steamer. Although he had taken the trouble to provide himself with a visa for Panama, the American authorities would not let him disembark at Cristobal, cross the road, and stay at a hotel in Colon. They insisted that if he once left *Mischief* he would have to go to a sort of local 'Ellis Island' and remain there until he embarked. To avoid this semi-imprisonment we transferred him to *Skaffie*'s crew list where he nominally lived until his ship arrived. However, authority made some amends for this piece of far-flung bumbledom by allowing me to buy provisions from the canal commissary, the canal employees' emporium for everything from food and clothing to children's toys.

On 1 May, having got our clearance papers, we sailed for Bermuda by way of the Yucatan channel and Florida straits. This route had been suggested by 'the Master', for unless one is going to call at the West Indies it is the best way for sailing ships to leave the Caribbean. Over this sea the north-east trades blow strongly, so that a yacht making for either the Windward Passage east of Cuba or the Mona Passage east of San Domingo must face a beat to windward of more than 700 miles.

For the first three or four days, sailing close-hauled with a wind of force four or five in a rough sea, none of us felt at our best. We had been wafted smoothly along by breezes from astern, or from abaft the beam, for too long to take kindly to windward sailing. We felt hardly used; our sympathies were entirely with the unknown fair one:

> Oh, for a fair and gentle wind:
> I heard a fair one cry:
> But give to me the snoring breeze
> And white waves leaping high.

The rotator of our patent log had been taken by a shark in the Gulf of Panama, and as we had been unable to get another in Colon we could only estimate the day's run; and each man as he came off watch entered in the log what he thought the ship had done in his watch. A sudden and unaccountable set of twenty-five miles to the east shook my own confidence as well as that of the crew in my calculations, and let loose a sustained outburst of star, planet, and moon shooting. I had wished to get well to windward of the Mosquito Bank and had perhaps allowed too much for leeway; this new position, however, enabled us to lay a better course direct for Cape San Antonio at the western end of Cuba. This brought the wind free and hereafter sailing became very pleasant.

On the 10th in a flat calm, and shortly before a tropical deluge opened on us, we sighted the Cape Antonio lighthouse. Before the current running north out of the Caribbean sets westwards as the Gulf Stream it enters and circles the Gulf of Mexico, so that if there is no wind a ship can only drift northwards. The next four days, until we got into the Gulf Stream proper, were exasperating and unrewarding. We drifted and sailed north almost into the Gulf of Mexico close to the Dry Tortugas, and then worked our way back again to the coast of Cuba not far from Habana. Going about, we once more headed north and presently we began to feel the effect of the stream. As we neared Florida the lights on its well-lit coast slid past us as though we were in a train. It had taken us a fortnight to get into the Gulf Stream, but it was worth it. Here, in the Florida Straits in the axis of the stream we got a lift of some seventy miles a day. Even well to the north of this we were enough under its influence to benefit to the extent of some forty miles a day.

Off the Florida coast we nearly always had several ships in sight, mostly tankers—even more traffic, I thought, than one would meet in the English Channel. Gulf Stream weather is notoriously unsettled. We experienced calms, light north-easterlies and some terrifying electrical storms with forked lightning stabbing the sky in all directions. A strong norther in the Gulf Stream, blowing as it would against the current, raises a short and irregular sea dangerous to small craft. Even in calm weather we saw some very queer tide rips and over-falls with stretches of smooth water between.

It might have paid us to have stayed in the Gulf Stream almost as far as Cape Hatteras before turning east for Bermuda; for when we quitted it in lat. 29° we met mainly contrary winds. On three successive days, although the glass rose steadily the whole time, we had winds of nearly gale force blowing straight at us from the direction of Bermuda.

At last, thirty days out from Cristobal, we sighted the islands. By evening we were close under Gibb's Hill lighthouse at the south-east end of Hamilton island. In the morning we were still there, for the wind had failed. Starting the engine we chugged quietly along, with the island close to port, admiring the scenery and criticising the ugly and abominably expensive hotels. Steering light-heartedly for the buoys marking the entrance to the channel through the reef, we neglected to check our position by cross bearing. Someone had just remarked upon the increasing paleness of the water when *Mischief* groaned twice and came protestingly to a standstill. Where was now our care-free mood? Crestfallen and with gnawing anxiety wc began to unlash the dinghy preparatory to running out a kedge anchor. But before we could launch it two grinning Bermudians came up in a motor boat to tell us they had been bawling themselves hoarse to warn us we were standing in to danger. More to the purpose they added that the tide was making. We got off soon after and followed them back to the channel a quarter of a mile away. After that humiliating experience we diligently picked up, identified, and ticked off in the *Pilot* every buoy— and there must be more than fifty—marking the long, tortuous channel to Hamilton Harbour, a distance of nearly twenty miles.

There are 360 islands or islets in the Bermudas but of these only twenty are inhabited or, one supposes, inhabitable. It is a pity that the people of Hamilton cannot be dispersed over some of the other 340. Although the houses are widely scattered—and very gay they are with their white-washed roofs, pink-washed walls, and windows picked out in blue or yellow—there is hardly a spot in the island which is not overlooked by a house or houses. Perhaps the blight which since the war has killed nearly all the trees (the so-called Bermuda cedar) partly accounts for this feeling of nakedness. The white-washed roofs are a singular feature. It is done, we were told, on account of the water. Rain water is the sole source of supply, and each house has an underground storage tank in which the water off the roof is collected. Whitewash is a panacea for a good many things, but does it purify water? Perhaps, as Tallulah Bankhead remarked, there is less in this than meets the eye.

The ban on motor traffic which had been operating up to the last war did not withstand for long the impact of war and the consequent opening of the American base. The ban might with advantage have been extended to include the harbour traffic where the peace of the many is destroyed by the few who tear round on water skis behind fast motor boats. The sight most worth seeing in Bermuda is the racing of the Bermuda 'fitted' dinghies. This is a class peculiar to Bermuda. The dinghies are 14ft. long. They have a 14ft. bowsprit and a boom which projects over the counter almost as far. They carry 500 square feet of sail and are manned by a crew of six or seven, every man of whom is needed, I imagine, to keep the boat upright and to help with the baling. In light winds it is permissible to jettison some of this human ballast.

In a few days we were ready to begin the last leg. The only major repair had been the welding and rebolting of the gammon iron which supports the bowsprit. Now that Michael had left, only Procter, George, and myself were available for watch-keeping, though John made it easier for us by taking a watch in the afternoon. We sailed on 7 June.

By great circle course the distance from Bermuda to the Scillies is 3353 miles. We did it in thirty-two days and for most of the way we had generous gales of wind and usually from a favourable direction. The passage was marked by a number of minor mishaps, attributable sometimes to our own folly or laziness and sometimes to the wearing out of the running rigging on the last few thousand miles of a twenty thousand mile voyage. The first, which might have been more serious, occurred a few days out early one morning in my watch. We had been running all night with whole mainsail and a twin boomed out. When I took over she was rolling and yawing wildly, but probably no more than she had been doing during the night. At length the gybe which I was beginning to fear happened. For a moment the wire boom guy held the boom high in the air; then it broke, and the boom crashed over wrapping the main sheet round the horse and breaking the back-stay tackle. The staysail was flat aback as well, so that when the crew tumbled up in response to my yell they were not a little startled by my new arrangements. With the mainsheet round the horse it was impossible for us to haul the boom inboard so that the sail could then be lowered. Taking a horribly rash decision I told them to stand by for another gybe. Back the boom came with a sickening crash, the main sheet unwound itself in a flash, and all was well. We then handed the mainsail, hoisted the twins, and felt much safer.

Next morning in a wild squall and at the inconvenient time of just before breakfast the sheet of one of the twins parted, and a few seconds later the cranse iron at the outer end of the other boom came adrift. We now had both sails streaming out ahead of the ship like washing on a line. We tamed them after a fierce struggle and fortunately before anything had been torn. The wind then moderated and a period of wet, misty weather succeeded these alarms. We accounted for the mist by our proximity to the tail of the Newfoundland Banks. From time to time we heard ship's foghorns and on one occasion, when a ship appeared suddenly out of the mist, George, who was apt to get excited, started waving his shirt. She was the *Lessel*, a Lamport and Holt boat in ballast. Possibly the look-out had mistaken George's shirt-waving for a distress signal, for she came in close enough to hail us by megaphone to ask if all was well. On our wireless set we could hear St John's giving out the weather forecast for the Grand Banks. A few days later a valve broke and we heard nothing more of weather reports or the much more important time signals. Since leaving Panama we had become accustomed to going without a log, and since Bermuda we had had no stop watch. It had been dropped in the bilge and had understandably given up. Throwing it overboard was fun. After this we dared not move the deck watch from its little brass bed in the cabin, so when taking sights I had to bawl out to someone below who noted the time.

Another depression soon caught up with us and for two days we sped—everything reefed right down—before a southerly gale. I judged we were doing 'twelve knots and a Chinaman', as the saying goes.* Anyhow we ran 350 miles (by sights) in two days while the great following seas took *Mischief* in their arms and hurled her forwards. In our enthusiasm we began shortening the passage by days or even weeks, but I deprecated too much optimism by enumerating all the accidents which might happen to us, including even the breaking of the boom. Sure enough the next day it did break.

That night the barometer dropped very steeply and at three in the morning it was blowing very hard and raining. As usual we had left the mainsail up for too long and no one fancied taking it down in such wild conditions in the dark. As she was going too fast for safety we streamed over the counter the bights of two of our heaviest warps to slow her down and then prayed for dawn. By morning,—it was Midsummer Day—the wind moderated and shifted to north-west. A big sea was running and the boom, which should have been hauled in and pinned amidships—for now there was scarcely enough wind to fill it— was slamming about. It had already broken the rope tail of its wire guy when I took over after breakfast. I at once noticed that it had a slight curve. Suspecting that it was sprung I was about to call all hands when it broke, fairly in the middle. We had not yet taken out the reefs, that is there were four or five rolls of canvas round the boom. Having got it inboard we managed to straighten the boom by

---

*   In the old days when the log was hove the reel from which the log line ran out (the time being taken with a sand-glass) was held by a man. Most log lines were only marked to record a maximum speed of twelve knots. The story is that in the sixties one of the famous clippers was travelling so fast that the man holding the reel—a Chinaman—was jerked overboard and lost.

means of the throat halyards, but unrolling the sail with the boom lying on the deck was quite a job. We cut off a couple of feet at each end of the boom where the fittings were attached and threw the rest overboard. It was a surprise to find that it was a hollow spar; those of us who had had to lift it by the topping lifts had always imagined it as being made of solid iron. Henceforth we used the mainsail without any boom. This arrangement increased our peace of mind and did not much diminish our speed.

Before the next depression overtook us (when racing across the Atlantic the object, I understand, is not to be left behind by a depression) we had three days of light easterly winds and enough sun to encourage bathing. As we were in the traffic lane we expected to see large numbers of ships; a less expected sight in mid-Atlantic was a turtle. When on watch at night I always liked to see the lights of ships. They gave me a feeling of companionship and an interest in making out their course, and whether we should have to advertise our presence with the Aldis lamp. On one occasion I cut it rather too fine. Having assumed that a steamer would pass us about a quarter of a mile off I saw no point in showing a light, but when it eventually became obvious that he was going to come very close indeed I felt it wiser to lie doggo rather than to startle him by showing the light suddenly at such close range. It was always possible that the helmsman might panic and spin the wheel the wrong way. When their bridge was passing our bowsprit someone saw us and a spotlight was directed down on to our deck together with a volley of abuse in some foreign tongue.

Towards the end of June there began a spell of dirty weather which was to last almost to the Scillies. Rain, high winds, and rough seas combined to make life wet and wearing. The companion way was boarded up, the hatch cover closed, the skylight battened down—but nevertheless water managed to find its way below. Although the helmsman was partly protected by the dodger rigged round the cockpit he still had the benefit of enough spray and solid water to keep him awake; and even the briefest of visits to the cockpit to survey the weather compelled one to be fully clothed. As one stood at the foot of the companion struggling into wet oilskins before going on watch, one would call hopefully to the helmsman for some words of comfort, for the least hint of a change for the better. But seldom were they forthcoming. Instead, more briefly and rudely worded, one heard:

> I tell you naught for your comfort,
> Yea, naught for your desire,
> Save that the sky grows darker yet
> And the seas rise higher.

The night of 29 June was particularly bad. The glass having fallen had apparently steadied. We had the trysail up and a twin boomed out. During the night the glass slumped to 29.2″ and at four in the morning, when we must have been doing seven knots, we had to hand the sails and run under storm jib alone. When daylight broke on a grey wilderness of white-capped waves we successfully experimented with a couple of oil bags trailing from either quarter. We found that even the finest film of oil had a remarkably soothing effect when angry waves tried to break close to our counter. Towards the close of a dark and dismal day a German ship altered course to see how we were faring. She came very close to us but signalling was impossible as we were more often out of sight in the trough of a wave than in view.

Discomfort can more easily be borne when one is being driven homewards with such vigour. Every day we ran our hundred miles or more, whether under storm jib alone or with the trysail and a twin. Opportunities for taking sights had to be promptly seized. They were not common and on two consecutive days we could not take any at all. However, on 5 July, in improving weather, we found ourselves only sixty miles from the Bishop rock. That night we picked up the light and by breakfast time on a lovely summer morning we were off St Mary's. A year and a day after leaving we passed Falmouth, but by now we were enveloped in dense fog. For three days as we groped our way up Channel the fog persisted. Because of the tide we anchored in home waters for the first time in Swanage Bay, but at last on 9 July we entered Lymington river and tied up at the yard where we had fitted out.

Next day the crew went their several ways and I was left once more to commune with *Mischief*. I will not pretend that at all times throughout this 20,000-mile voyage we were a band of brothers. Patient Griselda herself and a company of angels would sometimes find their tempers strained to breaking point when cooped up in a small ship for months together. 'Ships are all right—it's the men in them', was, I suspect, the thought of each one of us on many occasions; and I know for certain of a few occasions when the same idea was openly and more pointedly expressed. But we were old enough or sensible enough to bear and forbear, and to put the ship and the enterprise in hand before our own feelings. It was this loyalty to the ship, and not my management, that held the crew together and enabled us to bring a worthwhile undertaking to a successful end.

Record of earlier attempts to cross the ice-cap

(The list of expeditions briefly recorded here may not be complete)

In February 1914 Drs Cristobal Hicken and Frederico Reichert with two others landed near the foot of the Bismarck glacier on Lake Argentino. (At that time this glacier was called 'Moreno'). They reached a height of 5000 ft. and saw a glacier which appeared to lead to San Andres fjord, but bad weather obliged them to turn back.

In January 1916 Reichert and others made an attempt by the Viedma glacier which drains into Lake Viedma, some fifty miles north of Lake Argentine. They reached the ice-cap before bad weather stopped them.

In January 1921 Reichert and Hicken, with the assistance of the Chilean navy, landed on the San Rafael glacier on the Pacific side near the northern extremity of the ice-cap. They got within four miles of San Valentino before being driven back by the weather. In the same year the Swedish explorer Dr Nordenskjoeld, also assisted by the Chilean government who lent the tender *Yanez*, started from Kelly Bay in the north-east corner of the Gulf of Peñas. Nothing was achieved.

In 1931 Agostini went up the Upsala glacier which lies between lakes Argentino and Viedma. Having reach a point on the ice-cap whence they could see Falcon fjord they returned.

In January 1933 Reichert and Dr Neummeyer attempted to cross to Eyre Sound from Lake San Martino which is north of Lake Viedma. They reached the watershed but retreated after stormy weather had lasted for sixteen days. In the middle of the ice-cap they found an active volcano.

In 1939 Reichert and Captain Ihl made another unsuccessful attempt by the valley of the River Leon which drains into Lake Buenos Aires.

In 1940 the Swiss geologist Arnold Heim tried by the same route up the Leon valley west of Lake Buenos Aires. They reached the ice and recognised San Valentino fifteen miles to the north-west. Bad weather forced them to return.

In 1940 Reichert, Ihl, and several others, with half a ton of stores, started from Lake San Rafael on the Pacific side. They were out from January to April. Reichert and Ihl returned, but two of the party, starting on skis from a central depot in the neighbourhood of San Valentino, reached Lake Fiero at the head of the Leon valley, twelve miles from Lake Buenos Aires.

In 1954 Major Huerta, an Argentine army officer, is reported to have landed on Lake Argentino in sea-planes with a large well equipped party, and crossed the ice-cap to the Pacific. No details of the route are available.

Two Summers Before The Mast

Bob Comlay

THE VOYAGE TO PATAGONIA marked the first of twenty voyages to high latitudes in both hemispheres, undertaken in a succession of three former Bristol Channel pilot cutters. These travels, totalling some 160,000 miles, are documented with masterly understatement and typically dry humour in the eight volumes of Tilman's 'Sailing/Mountain Exploration' books.

I first met Bill Tilman when I was 17 years of age; he was 71, old enough to be my grandfather. By the time I was halfway through my nineteenth year I'd made two voyages north, sailing more than 10,000 miles and spending just over eight months at sea with him, 'taking the rough with the smooth', to quote his own stated requirement of me. If my late teenage years had turned out to be rather more full than for some of my peers, they paled in comparison with his. By the time Tilman had reached the age of twenty, he'd been twice to the Western Front, twice awarded the Military Cross, and twice wounded. A year later when the Great War was over, countless numbers of his peers had perished and he was already moving on to a new life in Africa. His extraordinary travels on that continent, his achievements in the high mountains of the Himalaya and his maverick activities behind enemy lines in the Second World War were all behind him by the time I was born. When I'd just turned two, he was already setting out on his first adventure under sail: the long haul down to Patagonia for a first crossing of the Patagonian icecap.

Small boat voyages across oceans and into high latitudes for months at a time required a crew with a blend of characteristics which were not easily found. With a working crew of four, single-handed watch-keeping on the ocean passages was a necessity in all but the most extreme weather, when double watches might be set. The crews of Tilman's pilot cutters therefore worked two hours on watch and six hours off, with the fifth member, the all-important cook, taking a single two-hour watch in the afternoon to enable rotation of the watch-keeping schedule. The cook's lighter load on deck reflected his responsibility for managing food and water supplies, producing regular meals from the most rudimentary of ingredients and preparing them in a cramped and uncomfortable galley. In each of Tilman's boats the cook had to rely upon paraffin-fuelled Primus stoves, preheated with methylated spirits soaked into a makeshift twisted wire and asbestos fibre wick. It was a tough job, for which a full night's sleep was a just reward.

Over the course of his sailing career Bill Tilman took on almost one hundred different crew members. Those with a background of mountaineering or the army were taken on trust—their loyalty under pressure and respect for his leadership never in doubt, even if their fitness for small boat voyages at times left something to be desired. Professional mariners applying, particularly merchant seamen looking for some 'real' small boat adventure, might be relied upon for their sea legs and their deep-sea experience. The remainder of the crews were selected through notices placed in suitable journals, typically in the personal column of *The Times*. These advertisements were deliberately worded along the lines of *Hands wanted for long voyage in small boat. No pay, no prospects, not much pleasure* in order to weed out the chaff. The mixed bunch of applicants that resulted included a number of young people like myself, the kind that we would probably now loosely term 'gap year' candidates.

It should be of little surprise that some of the applicants to these notices included young women to whom polite letters of refusal had to be written. Describing the response to an advertisement for a cook for the 1970 voyage, Tilman writes 'From the twelve possibilities I had little difficulty in choosing. After eliminating the two professionals out of hand, Georgina with reluctance, and one or two others who sounded odd, the remaining six, all but one, eliminated themselves. When I met him, although I did not tell him so, Andrew Harwich was the only candidate.'*

I made two voyages with Tilman in his second Bristol Channel pilot cutter *Sea Breeze*, the first to West Greenland in 1970, and the

---

*   *In Mischief's Wake*, H. W. Tilman, 1972

second to East Greenland in 1971. Looking back on these travels with the benefit of forty-five years of hindsight, the simplicity of Tilman's approach and the basic nature of the stores and equipment is worth highlighting.

Sea Breeze sailed with much the same gear as she had when originally launched by Bowden of Porthlevn in 1899. With the exception of a Terylene staysail, her working rig (of mainsail, topsail and jib) was of flax canvas. The running rigging was hemp, the standing rigging was wire, the shrouds tensioned with traditional deadeyes and lanyards rather than bottle-screws. There were no winches on any of the running rigging; all sail hoisting and trimming was carried out by sweating lines against belaying pins and deck cleats. In high latitudes, showers of tiny ice crystals would float down from the blocks as halyards were hauled, shimmering in the sunlight. Reefing the mainsail in a rising wind required two men, one on each of two crank handles attached to the original 'Appledore' roller reefing gear. In her working days, she would have been crewed by a man and a boy; clearly they were made of sterner stuff then. Under most points of sail, *Sea Breeze* would happily maintain a course with the tiller lashed for sufficient time to enable the man on watch to adjust the sail trim himself. Indeed, it became a regular diversion from the tedium of the night watch to lash the helm and allow her to sail herself so that as much time could be spent out of the cockpit as possible, watching the tracks of dolphins under the bowsprit and, on the passage home, the *aurora borealis*.

Off watch, the crew usually retired to their bunks, either to sleep, to write a journal or to lose themselves in a book. The Skipper, an avid reader, encouraged his crew to stow their personal collections in the saloon bookshelves, one of the few reliably dry storage areas on the boat. The resulting shared collection made for a curiously eclectic library which the Skipper worked through faster than the rest of us, delivering witty criticism with a mischievous grin over breakfast.

As mealtimes approached, the off-watch crew would start to gather round the saloon table, swapping stories and making unlikely plans inspired by our shared experience. With the staple diet of corned beef and dried vegetables starting to wear a little thin, shared culinary fantasies involving rare steaks and strawberries were common sources of light relief.

Sea Breeze was a fine sea-boat, but by no means a dry ship on the Atlantic crossings. A breaking sea would soon find its way through the rotten deck fastenings and on to the saloon table. To minimise this discomfort, a simple system of guttering was constructed from plastic fertiliser sacks suspended beneath the offending deck beam. An old enamel jug hung from a twisted wire strop at the lee end of the guttering, and in stormy weather the final task at the end of the watch, having written up the log, was to empty and replace the jug.

The auxiliary engine, a two-cylinder twenty-seven-horsepower diesel, had been fitted in the 1940s as an afterthought, with temperamental electrics and a curious arrangement of three fuel tanks which would contribute to her demise in 1972. We used the engine as little as possible, for when motoring the boat became virtually uninhabitable below due to the noise and the fumes. With her propeller offset to starboard, tight turns to port were possible but attempts to turn to starboard were unpredictable without well-timed bursts of reverse. If manoeuvring under engine in ice was challenging, in a modern marina it could be downright disastrous and it was for this reason that the only insurance cover that Tilman took out for his pilot cutters related to third parties in the Lymington River.

After the Walker patent log shed its spinner before we were out of the English Channel at the start of the 1970 trip, we soon became quite adept at estimating distance run to a fair degree of accuracy. Long before the modern convenience of radar and GPS chart plotters, navigation was by sextant with fixes plotted on a variety of paper charts of uncertain vintage. On the coast of Greenland the age of the charts mattered little, their accuracy in 1970 seeming at best rudimentary. For depth soundings we relied on a traditional lead-line, marked off in fathoms. We'd work our way into a potential fjord anchorage with one crew member heaving the lead and calling out the sounding while another held the anchor, ready to drop at the Skipper's command. Standing up in the bow in ice-strewn waters heaving and recovering the lead was a cold and wet pursuit. Navigation in the ice was a black art; while the sun was usually clear in the sky, the horizon was invariably obscured by ice or low fog banks. The deck watch, carefully and regularly wound by the Skipper alone, gave up the ghost in mid-Atlantic while his sextant, professionally maintained by the same shore-based cowboys who looked after the Walker log and the deck watch, offered a choice of three suns for the navigator to bring down onto a selection from three horizons.

With such basic tools and techniques one might have expected the results to be somewhat haphazard. On the contrary, in the course of four North Atlantic crossings the Skipper brought us in to a landfall with the expected waypoint 'under the bow', each time within a matter of a few hours of the predicted time. If his coastal navigation was sometimes lacking, his ocean passage navigation was uncannily accurate. It was for this proven skill that he was invited to join the schooner *Patanela* as skipper and navigator for the successful 1964 Australian Heard Island expedition, itself a remarkable feat of navigation.*

Long before the availability of satellite technology, these voyages were true adventures at the end of what might be termed the era of 'heroic' exploration. The destinations were remote, the ocean passages followed little-travelled courses and we sailed without lifejackets, safety lines or life-rafts. GPS locator beacons had yet to be invented and would, in any event, have been of little or no use; for much of the voyage, Tilman's boats were hundreds of miles beyond the normal range of rescue services. While this might now appear foolhardy, Tilman's attitude to safety was pre-emptive: wherever possible taking sensible measures to avoid getting into danger rather than taking uncalculated risks with either boat or crew. His argument, which none of us questioned, was that we should keep ourselves out of trouble rather than invite it aboard.

Bob Comlay
Crew member 1970 (West Greenland) & 1971 (East Greenland)
July 2015

---

*   *Mostly Mischief*, H.W. Tilman, 1966

H. W. TILMAN

The Collected Edition

For the first time since their original appearance, all fifteen books by H. W. Tilman are being published as single volumes, with all their original photographs, maps and charts. Forewords and afterwords by those who knew him, or who can bring their own experience and knowledge to bear, complement his own understated writing to give us a fuller picture of the man and his achievements. A sixteenth volume is the 1980 biography by J. R. L. Anderson, *High Mountains and Cold Seas*. The books will appear in pairs, one each from his climbing and sailing eras, in order of original publication, at quarterly intervals from September 2015:

www.tilmanbooks.com